G000130016

Decimal Currency for Britain

Decimal Currency for Britain

by D. Neville Wood

Ward Lock and Company Limited

7062 3600 9

Design: David Roberts

Filmset by Keyspools Ltd Golborne Warrington Lancs
in Monophoto Plantin 10 on 12 point

Impreso en los talleres de EDITORIAL FHER, S. A.
BILBAO (España)
PRINTED IN SPAIN

Contents

1	Introduction	7
2	This is not a new idea	11
3	How will it be better?	17
4	Learning from the other countries that have changed over	23
5	The £ versus the 10*s*	35
6	The new coins	49
7	The change-over	54
8	We already use the decimal	59
9	Wanted: a thousand beer bottle tops	64
10	On to a full metric system	74
	Decimal quiz	77
	Conversion tables	83
	Bibliography	87
	Index	89

Introduction

The transition to a decimal currency in Britain is planned to take place early in 1971. We have known that this was becoming increasingly likely for several years, and, in accepting in principle the main recommendations of the Halsbury Committee[1], the Government prepared the way for the announcement in March 1966 that this country would be making the great change-over to a decimal currency in February 1971. Included in the Chancellor's announcement was the decision to accept the majority recommendation of the Halsbury Committee, by 4 to 2, that the major unit of our currency would continue to be the £.

We also know now that 'D-day'—a phrase I should like to use throughout this book to denote the date of the change-over to a decimal currency—has been firmly fixed. The actual date in February 1971 has not yet been determined, but if the precedent of South Africa and Australia holds good, then a Monday in the middle of the month, probably the 15th must be a likely choice.

It is already apparent that this will not be without its problems, objections and difficulties, and it is to meet some of these objections and to try to alleviate some of these anxieties that this book is written. This does not mean, however, that my approach is going to be negative, for I regard the benefits and advantages of a decimal currency as far more important and long-lasting than the transient difficulties which may precede and accompany the actual change-over.

One or two points must be made clear therefore at the start. Firstly that I am the headteacher of a junior school, and my views and opinions must obviously be coloured by the effects this great change will make on life in the classroom. I have read the Halsbury report on decimal currency in much the same way that you might treat a highly-esteemed novel, marking relevant phrases, underlining particularly telling passages, making notes in the margin and deleting some of the details which no longer apply or recommendations which were not

[1] Report of the Committee of Enquiry on Decimal Currency: HMSO 1963

accepted. Most of its 254 pages have some marks. The more recent White Paper[1] can be assimilated very rapidly.

I have interested myself for a long time in this subject, and have written and lectured about it. I can claim therefore to have come up against many, if not all of the questions that this controversial topic can evoke. My audiences have mainly been teachers and parents, and I have naturally spoken to them directly and informally; I should like to retain something of this approach as I write, so my second introductory point is a request to regard this book as an informal conversation. Since this talk will be a little long and one-sided, I shall try to anticipate, as far as possible, the sort of questions that would arise in discussion. I shall be expressing some opinions and convictions with which you may agree or disagree. This is inevitable with a subject like this.

But, although I shall have my teaching colleagues in mind as I write, I am particularly keen to write for a much wider public. Whether we like the idea or not, we are all going to be involved. In fact, there is hardly a topic as universal in its effect as that of the coins in our purses, the banknotes in our pockets and the cheques in our wallets. My wife will have to cope with shopping with decimal coins and my children will want pocket-money . . . and that means decimal coins too.

It is, therefore, going to be no small change for all of us. If you think of the advent of decimalization as a rather puzzling and tiresome piece of government legislation, I hope that by the time you come to the end of these pages you may have changed your mind.

At the time of writing, we are still awaiting some of the details of the final system. The Decimal Currency Board has been set up and will be making recommendations to the Chancellor of the Exchequer on such problems as the names of the new coins, the questions of possible limited compensation for the inevitable losses which the change-over will mean for shops and businesses, the exact date for 'D-day', and when some of our existing coins—particularly the halfpenny will be demonetized—i.e. will no longer be legal tender. We ask your indulgence therefore if by the time this book is in your hands, some of the details turn out to be slightly different. I hope any necessary corrections and alterations can be put right in future editions and suggest that you might like to draw my attention to any such changes, by writing to me through the publishers.

In my research I have contacted many companies, organizations and interested individuals and have already thanked them for their helpful advice and comments. To thank them all again in print would be both lengthy and

[1] Decimal Currency in the United Kingdom: HMSO Cmnd 3164

risky. The risk lies in that I am sure to omit someone who has been really helpful, so no list of names is included here. However, I must thank the officials in the Information Offices of the South African Embassy and the High Commissioner's Office in London of both the Australian and New Zealand Governments not only for their help, but for permission to quote from relevant writings. I am also grateful to the National Union of Teachers for permission to quote in full the Memorandum of Evidence that they submitted to the Committee of Enquiry on Decimal Currency in 1962.

I am also relieved to learn that reasonable quotations can be made from HMSO publications with due acknowledgment; not that I have deliberately taken large slices from either the Halsbury Report or the White Paper, but simply because some of the phraseology must inevitably have been consciously or subconsciously registered in my mind, and may well reappear in subsequent chapters.

After you have read this book you may like to test your grasp of the implications of this subject by working through the Decimal Quiz which is included at the end of the book. The answers are all to be found in the text of the book so please don't send them to me for marking!

Finally, if this book itself feels or looks unusual in some way, this may be because of its measurements. It seemed appropriate that it should be produced to a *metric* specification—the size of sheet (A5, 148mm × 210mm) is one of the sizes recommended by the International Organization for Standardization.

This is not a new idea

The decision to change our currency to a decimal based system has been called a historic one. But nobody can say that we have not taken our time in coming to this conclusion. Many would attribute this to our native caution, our love of tradition and our suspicion of change. Others might say, with equal conviction, that our delay and reserve, our insularity or our position in past years in world trade have all resulted in this belated, expensive and complicated operation and that we might have avoided this upheaval if we had taken a firm decision fifty or a hundred years ago, as many other nations did.

There are plenty of good books already on the history of money, on coin-collecting, on banking, finance and number systems. Some of these are listed in the bibliography, but I feel that most of these considerations are outside the scope of this book. But since some of them are directly concerned with the development of the decimal and its use in money systems throughout the world, we ought to look at some of these developments as a background to the present revolution in our coinage.

'The biological accident of our having ten fingers' . . . is how one of the earliest paragraphs in the Halsbury Report describes the use of ten as a basis for counting. If it wasn't for this, we might just as readily be counting in eights, twelves or twenties. This built-in ready reckoner plays a part in the development of most of the early number systems. The stress which is laid upon the giving of tithes—'One-tenth unto the Lord'—as far back as Abraham and its subsequent incorporation into the Law of Moses will be sufficient to underline it as, at least, an approved and useful standard of measurement from early days. We might note the early connections between money and weight—the shekel, the basic Hebrew coin, was also a measure of weight. We find the tenth appearing in other ways—in dry weight, the omer was a tenth part of the ephah and many other reckonings were either decimal or a combination of the decimal system with the Babylonian sexagesimal system—sixty minutes in the hour, for example. That these measures have survived the centuries is an interesting testimony to the usefulness and importance of ten in calculations of all sorts. Here again, I do not want to enter on controversial ground, but in choosing my examples from Jewish civilization, I am not only selecting a system which spans the centuries, but have focussed attention on a culture which is certainly not inconspicuous in modern financial acumen. Perhaps this is not entirely due to the decimal point, but it is a more forceful argument to me than a selection of ideas from dead civilizations or ancient customs.

Coming closer to our own day we can observe the efforts, largely unsuccessful until now, to establish a decimal currency in this country. It would be very interesting to read the reactions of teachers and parents of 1824 when a House of Commons motion declared itself in favour of a change to decimal coinage, always supposing that angry letters were written to *The Times* on this issue.

How did we react in 1841? Were there strong feelings expressed when a Royal Commission agreed with this recommendation? And what happened in 1849 when people first handled the florin? Here we have, for the first time, a coin specially introduced to pave the way towards a decimal coinage, and even inscribed 'one-tenth of a pound' from 1849 to 1887. I suspect that there was more fuss over the omission of the words 'Dei Gratia' from this new coin —hence its nickname, the 'godless florin'—than over the novelty of having a first decimal coin, or over the origin of its name from the city of Florence.

Certainly no one in power in 1853 felt sufficiently moved to take any positive action when a Select Committee in that year came out in favour of the decimal. If they had done so, we should not now be thinking of how much time and energy we have dissipated on an archaic currency over the past hundred years.

If the opponents of decimalization kept quiet in 1853, did they welcome with bursts of acclamation, the findings of yet another Royal Commission four years later, in 1857? Then it was recommended that it was not desirable to disturb the habits of the people in the matter of the coinage of the realm.

Did the teachers of 1868, going to work in many a 'new' village school— this is the date on the gable-end of the village school where I was headmaster previously—bewail the fact that another Royal Commission had said 'No' to the decimal? It certainly looks as if the mid-Victorians were undecided on the subject. Perhaps nobody really thought any more about the idea until Queen Victoria had been on the throne for fifty years, when it was decided that it would be a good plan to issue a 4*s* piece, a huge double florin, to commemorate her golden jubilee. Probably because of its weight and size it did not survive and coin catalogues show the dates 1887–1890 only. It may have been designed by a keen decimal man with an idea for which we were not ready, for it is not until 1918 that another enquiry is held, only to decide that the *status quo* should be preserved. This may not have been the best time to think about such a change, since the 'enemy' had a decimal currency, and so it is hardly surprising that we stuck to our four-twelve-twenty method of calculating.

There had been other Conferences with this topic on the agenda; the Colonial Conferences of 1902 and 1907 and the Imperial Conference in 1911 produced no positive results.

I must confess that I cannot recall any champion arising to the cause in 1951, when a Board of Trade Report on Weights and Measures included a favourable view on decimalizing the currency. But perhaps I can plead that I was not, at that time, so interested in the subject, although I had begun to discover just how difficult it was, and still is, for children of seven and eight to master our peculiar system.

No wonder the White Paper uses the phrase 'the early disenchantment with mathematics' in speaking of the processes of learning money-sums as tedious, time-consuming and lacking in intellectual excitement. We shall return later to the effects of the change on teaching techniques, timetables and textbooks, but it is fitting to say at this point that the White Paper is very well written, and it is a pity that the author(s) of this well-phrased and concise document must remain in the administrative anonymity required by the Civil Service.

Then, in 1960, a joint report by committees set up by the British Association for the Advancement of Science, and the Association of the British Chambers of Commerce indicated that there was considerable and growing interest in, and support for a change; this caused the setting up of many similar committees and study groups, most of which have registered willingness to change to a decimal system over a wide field of business and other organizations and trades.

By this time, plans were already well in hand for South Africa to change over to a decimal system. They had previously operated an *£-s-d* currency very similar to our own. As we shall see later, the way in which a successful conversion was made in South Africa has made people think again, or think more seriously about having a similar system in this country. If either South Africa, or the more recent transition of Australia and New Zealand had produced serious misgivings or doubts, perhaps we should not now be so keen; but their experiences only serve to underline the advantages, and show that the problems raised by the change-over are largely transitory or exaggerated, and can be met by sensible preparation, good publicity and staff training.

Unlike many of the earlier enquiries, the Halsbury Committee was not asked to enquire whether decimalization of our currency was desirable or not. When Mr Hugh Gaitskell, then the leader of the opposition, asked Mr Selwyn Lloyd, then Chancellor of the Exchequer, whether or not the Government had made a decision in principle in the matter, he was told that the Government felt that real advantage would follow from the adoption of a decimal currency. It became clear from this question in the Commons, at the time of the Chancellor's announcement of the appointment of the Halsbury Committee, that the question was not 'whether?' but 'how?' This Committee was, in fact, asked to advise on the most convenient and practical form which a decimal currency might take, including the major and minor units to be adopted; to advise on the timing and phasing of the change-over best calculated to minimize the cost; and, with these two earlier terms of reference in mind, to estimate the probable amount and incidence of the cost to the economy. I am not going to digress into how they fulfilled this, but it is worthwhile noting that in the 18 months during which they met from January 1962 to July 1963, they held no less than 57 meetings, dealt with almost 600 letters, took into account written evidence from almost 200 organizations, heard oral evidence from 35, and had the help of no less than 150 machine companies in the costing work. Obviously the visible evidence in their report is like the tip of the iceberg over the water-line in comparison with the mammoth task of sifting all the evidence and forming judgments based on all the accumulated testimony of so many interested parties.

The Committee had six members who were unanimous on all recommendations except the vexed question of the best unit to adopt. Four, in the majority report, felt that the £ was the best choice as the major unit; the other two produced a minority report, a Memorandum of Dissent, on this issue, in which they expressed their reasons for preferring the 10*s* unit.

Among the many organizations submitting evidence, was the National Union of Teachers. I am grateful to the NUT for permission to quote in full the Memorandum of Evidence they submitted in June 1962:

> If a decimal system of coinage were introduced there would be considerable saving in terms of teaching hours and individual effort on the part of both teacher and taught. In fact, time saved in the teaching of early groups, although considerable, might well be doubled for the children of 9–11 years of age, at which time they are acquiring the basic skills in the manipulation of money values.
>
> Arithmetical processes such as mechanical exercises and problems using the four rules in the use of money could be more quickly mastered. Similarly, with conversion and reduction, the keeping of accounts of all kinds and the working of fractions and percentages, some of the time saved for the arithmetic periods could, at the primary stage at least, be used for developing and expanding mathematical experience, as well as for improvement in the use of the mother tongue, both written and spoken, for which there can never be too much time. More time for the introduction of the foundation work in science could be found and the task itself would eventually be made easier by the introduction

> of the metric system of weighing and measuring. Indeed it would probably be easier for the schools if both changes could be introduced simultaneously.
>
> The biggest problem in so far as the schools are concerned would be the replacement of textbooks. This could possibly be achieved by granting a once-for-all capitation allowance for each child, equal to, say, a year's allowance. It might be desirable that this grant should come direct from the Exchequer, as it would be an unfair additional burden to place on the authorities who might otherwise be tempted or forced to make the necessary expenditure at the expense of other subjects.
>
> The preparation and introduction of the new textbooks would probably take two or three years at least. This necessary delay suggests that there should be *at least* three years' notice given of any intention to make the change.
>
> There would, of course, be some transitional difficulties for the schools, but these would not be serious and would only apply to the children in the schools at the time the change was made. For children, part of the confusion could arise from difficulties they might experience at home. Today this is less serious than it might have been—the ubiquitous television set will no doubt play its part in introducing both home and school to at least the mechanics of the new arithmetic simultaneously. Such initial difficulties as might arise would be far outweighed by the domestic, international and ultimate educational advantages to be derived from such a change.

I would only quibble with one sentence in the memorandum. From my experience and observation I think it would be disastrous to introduce both a new currency and a full metric system *simultaneously*. Certainly, I hope that the change-over to decimal currency is going to be the first step to a full metric system, but it would, I think, be most unwise to convert more than one major measure at a time. I shall be looking at the prospects of such a development in the final chapter. This ultimate aim is supported by the White Paper, which stresses that the full educational benefits of a decimal currency will only be obtained in conjunction with a full metric system of weights and measures.

We are nearly up to date with our history lesson now, before we embark on the more doubtful field of prophecy. However, many a prediction is based on the observation of the outcome of similar past situations, and with so many positive leads from recent history, and from so many other countries, I do not feel that this is too mystical an exercise.

In 1962 Eire also joined the list of countries who intended turning over to the decimal. They may only be waiting to see just what happens in this country before they too make a firm decision to go ahead with the change-over.

This means that well over 95% of the civilized world bases its currency on some form or other of a decimal unit. This would seem to be proof enough that the scheme is sound, and that it would be foolish if, after all this delay, we found ourselves still the only major country in the world without the benefits of decimal currency. It would be sad if we found ourselves clinging sentimentally to a tradition that is clumsy, archaic, insular and often aggravating to both ourselves and to foreigners, just because, for a short while, we might find life in the supermarket, the office or the classroom a little complicated.

You may think that in this quick historical survey I have forgotten our neighbours, who have had a decimal currency since the end of the eighteenth century, France. Other interested people have already appreciated the lessons we might learn by looking at a French maths book. For more than 150 years this has been their system and if you can get hold of a copy of either of the two volumes of *Calcul : Première et Deuxième Années,* with the bright companion book *Le Calcul Quotidien,* you will be able to sample for yourselves, in everyday examples of French shopping expeditions etc, the sort of approach that *they* have enjoyed for so long. What Zamenhof dreamed of for Esperanto as an international language seems to be eclipsed by this number ten, which, whether we think it is the best choice or not, has become the next-best thing to a universal language for money.

My apparent neglect of the French is only deliberate in the sense that I think it is more relevant to look carefully at the teaching methods, textbooks, timetabling of maths etc, in another English-speaking country. This I have been able to do, and I shall be describing later the results of looking into this question in Canada some years ago, before decimalization was a really live issue here, but at a time when I was hoping that some useful facts could be collected on the advantages of having such a system for ourselves.

How will it be better?

Picture, if you will, a little boy or girl of seven or eight, newly arrived at the junior school . . . no longer by definition a 'mixed infant'.

If you are a teacher this could be almost any one of the many ordinary children in the class—not one of the extraordinary children who are very bright, and not one of the slower ones still having difficulties with simple numbers—but just an average pupil, if there is such a thing, in a first-year junior class.

If you are a parent, please imagine your son or daughter in this situation, announcing with pride that teacher says we are going to do *money* sums this week.

If you are neither teacher nor parent, please try and cast your mind back to the time when this imaginary child might have been *you*—back to your days as a seven year-old, with all those new experiences crowding in on your receptive mind.

The background to our picture is as follows: in the infants', probably with the aid of lots of interesting and colourful aids, rods and other apparatus, you have discovered some of the properties and relationships of those numbers from one to nine, and some of the peculiar propensities of zero. You wrote down the symbols for these digits, slowly mastering not only the different shapes but the meaning behind the signs. You didn't call it 'place-value' in those days, but you discovered a way of carrying over from one column to the next. You discovered the 'tens-box', and 'carrying', and this was not only demonstrated and explored, but practised and mastered. You found out that a '1' followed by a '4' meant 'one ten and four units' and that it was called 'fourteen'. You may have gone on from this and learned what happened when there were three numbers . . . such as 456; this you knew was four hundreds, and five tens (fifty) and six units.

You became very confident about this, and perhaps went on to explore the realm of the thousand. It was very satisfying to play with these big numbers, because you knew that the same rule applied all the way along—even if you wanted to talk about millions. Every time there were ten in one box you changed them for one in the next . . . and so on. The beauty of this was that it worked in subtraction sums too. Likewise for multiplication and division—you were either involved in taking a ten from next door, or carrying one into the next place. It was all really quite easy, once you had the idea of the ten.

This delightful scene is about to be shattered; the bubble is about to be pricked by a cruel system that 'doesn't obey the rules'. Poor child—he is about to learn about 'pounds, shillings and pence' (and halfpennies).

Maybe you think that I am overpainting the picture? Could this be, possibly, that you have, through tears and sweat and somebody else's infinite patience managed to overcome this hurdle, and can now juggle with columns of figures with ease? Bear with me, for I want you to imagine the expression, so familiar to many of us teachers, that appears like a little cloud on the face of many a child when we have to say, 'Yes, it does come to thirteen pennies, but . . . that is not one shilling and *three* pennies over, it's only one shilling and *one* penny.'

This is only the beginning of what the White Paper calls the 'early disenchantment' which children experience in mastering this process of learning the skills necessary to the understanding of money.

In a sentence, then, the first and most far-reaching effect of turning over to a decimal coinage will be the harmonization of money and ordinary numerical calculations—in a word, 'simplification'.

It follows therefore, whether we think in terms of the office or the schoolroom, the bank or the shop, that ultimately, all our money calculations are going to be easier and quicker. Fewer irritating and time-consuming errors will creep in and this is very important. In determining which is the best method of teaching some mathematical processes in schools, especially in subtraction, one of the most important criteria is 'Which is least prone to error?' I am sure this will be an impressive argument for teachers who are looking forward to the benefits of the new coinage.

In most cases, too, there will be economy of paper, and the simplicity which flows from having a two-tier system, rather than a three-tier. We shall replace our present 'Pounds, shillings and pence' with 'Pounds and newpence', *not* with a three-tier system which requires an intermediary unit of account such as 'Pounds, florins and newpence'.

Many of our money transactions involve not only the payment for goods and services but also the giving and receiving of the correct change. Here again a few moments' reflection will prove that the simplification of the coinage must result in easier and quicker payment and change giving. This will not happen immediately, but once we are established in thinking in terms of the new coins and not mentally translating everything into the old money first, we shall all notice the difference.

From this streamlining of the teaching of all the four rules of money and reduction and conversion of money, this 'early disenchantment' should soon be replaced by a continuing confidence in the ability of a young child to make steady and measurable progress by carefully graded examples of increasing difficulty until a noticeably higher standard of work, both in output and complexity, should be attainable, well before the age of transfer to the secondary school.

Alongside this extra confidence to achieve more in quality and in quantity in mathematics, will be the extra time for all those other things for which, in a progressive junior school at least, there never seems to be enough time. The Memorandum of Evidence from the NUT mentioned earlier, draws attention to the opportunity this will afford for the improvement in the use of the mother tongue, both spoken and written. There is much stimulating, expressive and original work going on in many schools in the fields of creative writing and the prospect of having some extra time for the development of this necessary ability, is surely one which many teachers will be delighted to avail themselves of. When I speak of 'creative writing', it might just be that I am talking of the subject closest to your heart, but, for many other members of staff, there will already be thoughts of 'more time for music'—'extra art lessons' 'another hour for rural studies'—'let's start teaching them French, in the *lower*-junior classes as well'. In fact, there will be the enthusiasts in every subject and skill who will be eager to suggest to the headmaster that this or that *must* now have priority. The hours in the school day fly by, and the school year passes so quickly that the prospect of even another hour a week to use as we might wish is exciting and challenging.

But we do not really need to look beyond the realm of mathematics to find scope for this extra time. So much that is new is being explored in present-day mathematics; many children are learning concepts which we have never come across and which we have to keep abreast of. New bases for number work, individual research in sets, the widening use of structural apparatus of all sorts—in all of these the horizons are being pushed back. We should be able, in the schools, to develop these skills further, and shall find that the move towards decimalization will fit in admirably with these new approaches and concepts.

I think the Halsbury Committee were rather cautious in estimating the time saved in putting this no higher than 5% to 10% of maths teaching time, or 2% of the total teaching time. It is not an easy thing to estimate but I hardly think an hour a week as an estimate is either rash or presumptuous. On this I have been able to arrive at some tentative conclusions by talking to teachers and administrators in Canada. I was able to look at the work in the different grades, and this was more meaningful than it might be over here, since timetables and curricula are more rigidly laid down in the American continent.

With less room for experimentation, the yearly grades are more definitive of what shall be included in each stage. This might not suit many a British teacher, but it certainly makes it easier to find out what is being taught and when. I was favourably impressed with the ability of average Canadian children to manipulate their money problems with more certainty at, say, the age of ten, than some children over here. There seemed fewer pages in the textbooks devoted to detailed practice in the 'steps' of mastering money, and so the attainment of a reasonable facility in this must, I feel, be less time-consuming and complex. On this point, whilst thanking those who helped me in Canada, during a short stay there, I should appreciate informed comment on this not only from teachers in the American continent but also from teachers who have lived through the transition period in South Africa, Australia and New Zealand. I should think that this also might serve to confirm my opinion about time and effort saved, as the reports received from official sources in those countries makes this very clear.

Mention has already been made of the simplification of school textbooks and the anxiety expressed about where the money is going to come from to replace these obsolete textbooks, to buy new ones, and to replace apparatus and equipment geared to a dead currency.

This anxiety is underlined by the restrictions which the Government seem to intend placing on any recommended compensation. You will have noted that the NUT thinks that a year's capitation allowance in a lump sum would be a good way of meeting the necessary costs. It is to be hoped that the Chancellor has not overlooked this question and that some plans can be formulated by which this additional cost does not fall, through the local authorities, on the ratepayer, already heavily burdened in meeting part of local education expenditure. In their evidence to the Halsbury Committee, the Publishers' Association estimated that over 2,000 books would need revision costing about £1,300,000.

The weakness of this argument is that it assumes that all these books would be worth revising and reissuing. I should imagine that, for many an outdated maths book on publishers' shelves, decimalization may very well be the last nail in the coffin. Bear in mind also that the whole of a textbook does not become useless when all the money sums, and the answers that match these examples need changing. Not so long ago, teachers had to decide on making internal alterations to examples and answers in many textbooks when the farthing disappeared. This operation will be nothing like as simple as dropping farthings, but the number of books that will repay revision in this way may be comparatively small. Sample questioning of two Local Education Authorities' spending on books revealed that in one case 75% of books ordered referred to 9 titles only; with the other LEA, out of 400 titles ordered in a year, 25 titles accounted for one-third of all the books ordered in the year.

I am not seeking to minimize the impact which this problem of obsolete textbooks will have, and I recognize that this will be a greater problem for secondary schools and for colleges and universities than for primary schools both in regard to the cost of more detailed, and sometimes better-bound, books and the life-expectancy of these textbooks. This however, tends to ignore the wide discrepancy that already exists in the amount of money which many primary schools are allocated in comparison with their secondary school neighbours. The older child is better able, and more likely to look after his textbooks than his younger brothers and sisters, and in the primary schools we are accustomed to books being well-used over a comparatively short period, and then to be in need of replacement by some more modern set, or occasionally by the renewal of a particularly useful series.

By 1971, therefore, many of our mathematics textbooks will need replacing anyway, and headteachers will already be planning these needs, and estimating how much longer some books will last, and if, in some classes at least, it will be worth 'hanging on' and getting a completely new set of books for the school year 1970–71.

It is also true, that, apart from this built-in obsolescence, that publishers of educational textbooks have naturally been reluctant to embark on the production of new maths textbooks, not just because of the impending revisions that would be needed, but also because of the great changes which are taking place in thinking about mathematics teaching as a whole. Even now, there must be a further hiatus until the exact names of the coins and the acceptable abbreviations for them are publicized. I don't think there will be any shortage of suitable material when we know what these proposals are. You should be able to anticipate this a little, if you wish, as I shall describe in some detail, suggestions for introducting a decimal currency, with graded work cards, later in the book. The simplification of which we have spoken has been proved in action with juniors from 7 to 11, and I am very confident that they will make the necessary change-over without much difficulty when the time arrives.

So, do not despair if you feel that this is all a little frustrating, and that it bristles with difficulties which you might prefer to avoid. During a recent television interview on this topic, it was suggested that the children might pick this up quite quickly, and then go home and explain it to Mum and Dad. I think the interviewer might be quite near the truth.

These transitional difficulties will only arise in school for comparatively few children. Those who have passed the junior stage will probably have no more difficulty in adjustment than most adults, as they will be sufficiently mature to see the reasonings and the relationships involved. For the very young, who will start school in the next couple of years, no problems should arise, as they will have a fresh start . . . they will have nothing to 'unlearn'—and should be able to benefit straightaway from the ease of a system which has the same rules for ordinary numbers, as it does for money calculations. This, I think, brings us back to the picture with which we started this chapter.

Learning from the other countries that have changed over

Soon we shall all be issued with little booklets, conversion cards to help explain the new money, leaflets, diagrams, and the whole range of publicity material which is a necessary part of such a revolutionary move as a change in currency. As I write I have around me a considerable amount of the publicity material that was issued by South Africa, by Australia and by New Zealand. I am grateful to the London officials of these Governments for sending me so much useful data. This, together with sets of coins in the new decimal currency of these countries and a large pile of press-cuttings on this subject form the background to this chapter.

For the purposes of this survey, I shall not be including comment on some of the smaller countries that have recently decided to decimalize their currency, because their experiences are virtually identical with these three territories. Among these are Commonwealth countries—Aden 1951, Cyprus and the British West Indies (Eastern Caribbean) 1955; these were followed two years later by India, and more recently, in 1961, Pakistan made the change.

We shall be looking at the advantages and disadvantages of the 10*s* unit, in comparison with the recommended £ unit in the next chapter. But this is not a consideration which can easily be limited in this way, because it is relevant not only to this chapter—for all these three countries opted for the 10*s* unit, but it must recur in the chapter on coinage, on the problems of transition, and in suggesting ways in which this can already be tried out in schools with 'dummy' coins. It is important to mention this here especially as we look at relative price values, and the conversion details from old to new currencies in these three countries. For example under the £-unit system which *we* shall be using, 10 newpence (10 cents, if you like) will be equivalent to one-tenth of a pound, i.e. a *florin*; but, in South Africa and the other two countries which we are considering in this chapter, 10 cents is equal to one *shilling*.

South Africa had been using a currency similar to our own as far back as 1825, but since the end of the Second World War the question of a move to decimal currency had been under consideration.

The South African Government appointed the Becklake Committee to investigate this possibility, the work of which was subsequently taken over by a Committee of the Bureau of Standards and in 1954 this Committee produced a report on its findings, which was favourable towards change-over.

The third stage, the Decimal Coinage Commission, indicated by its name that South Africa was seriously intending to switch to the new system, and when, in August 1958 after two years' work, the Commission also concluded that this would be desirable, the Government was not slow to act on their recommendations.

By December of 1958 it was announced that a decimal system would be introduced within a short time; this proposal was not only going to affect South Africa but included the territory of South West Africa, and the three British Protectorate Territories of Bechuanaland (now independant as Botswana), Basutoland (Lesotho) and Swaziland. The trade links, relative geographical positions and other local economic factors made it desirable that these should also be included.

This decision was made effective by the passage of the Decimal Coinage Act in June 1959, and, as we have already mentioned, it was the 10*s*-cent system that had been recommended by their Decimal Coinage Commission which was adopted. We may notice here that South Africa implemented their decision in a little over 18 months from the passage of the Bill, for their 'D-day' was fixed for February 14th 1961. Compare this with the period of 'notice' we have been given, which will be almost 5 years from the announcement, to implement these proposals (March 1966 to February 1971), or over 4 years from the issue of the White Paper (December 12th 1966) to our own 'D-day'.

The South African coinage is called Rand and cents. Rand is denoted by a capital '*R*' (the plural is the same, 'Rand' not 'Rands') and the familiar '*c*' for cents. Only in Afrikaans is the plural the same as the singular—'cent'.

One important feature of South Africa's conversion, in which it differs not only from the transition in Australia and New Zealand but also from our own planned change-over, is that the old South African silver £-*s*-*d* coins were merely adapted to equivalent values under the new decimal system as a temporary measure. Entirely new coins were introduced only for the bronze cent and half-cent pieces in 1961. The full implementation of the decimal coinage in South Africa did not in fact take place until 1965–6 when a completely new range of decimal currency was gradually introduced. This new currency is described on pages 27 and 33–4.

For their first new decimal currency South Africa planned gold coins for 1 Rand and 2 Rand equivalent to 10*s* and £1 respectively—not for general circulation but for collectors. Five different silver coins and three bronze were also planned. The silver coins were to be 50 cents (crown), 20 cents (florin), 10 cents (1*s*), 5 cents (6*d*) and a coin worth threepence in their old values, with the new title of 2½ cents. To replace the low-value coins, there were to be cents, half-cents, and quarter-cents (worth 1·2*d*, 0·6*d* and 0·3*d* respectively).

We must observe that South Africa did not, in adopting the 10*s* unit, take the opportunity to rid herself of the fractional coin immediately, in fact we find an extra one being introduced in the 2½ cent piece. This is surprising, since one of the main reasons advanced by supporters of the 10*s* system is that it makes it possible to have a fully-decimalized currency, that is, having no fractional coins at all.

The old threepenny piece (the tickey, as the South Africans called it) was a more popular coin than the 2½ cent coin by which it was at first replaced. The new coin was unacceptable to many because of the difficulties which arose with such a coin in paying for goods and services, and in change giving. More errors are likely to occur with a coin like this than with a conventional half-penny.

I am sure that the experience gained by studying the effects of conversion in South Africa and now Australia, followed by New Zealand is extremely valuable. Not only does it point out the many advantages but it highlights some of the snags, both anticipated and unforeseen, from which we can profit in making our transition as smooth and as acceptable as possible.

It quickly became clear to the South African government that there was going to be no real need for a quarter-cent and none were minted. No 25 cent piece replaced the old half-crown when this was later withdrawn, since it was felt that, with a 20*c* piece worth a florin, no coin so close in weight and size would be necessary.

You may have noticed that I am using the phrase 'South Africa' throughout. This avoids any confusion about the country's status, since it was in this same year—1961—that the Union of South Africa withdrew from the British Commonwealth and became a Republic. It is understandable, therefore, that in designing their new coins the effigy of the Queen's head was omitted. Instead the effigy of Jan von Riebeeck, a pioneer settler, appears on the new coins and also on the new notes. Their new notes only differed from the old in this respect, apart from the change from pounds to twice the number of Rand.

The danger inherent in this system in which low-value coins are very nearly equivalent to the old values, tends to make many people think that the difference is not significant. This must be seen as a disadvantage of the 10*s* unit wherever it is adopted. This was underlined by the decision to issue the new bronze coins, 1 cent and ½ cent, with the same weight and size as the old penny and halfpenny. Our own White Paper points out the risks in this, not just of confusion during any transition period, but also the temptation it provides to the dishonest to use the lower-value coins in slot-meters etc.

I am not suggesting that this happened in South Africa, but this similarity of price tags did mean that some price increases could be more easily concealed. The South African Government was alive to this tendency and set the example itself, by bringing down the internal air-letter rate from 4*d* to 3*c* (3·6*d*), a 10% drop. This did not prevent some price rises, such as in newspapers, which, though seemingly trivial, amount to quite a lot by the time this small increase is added on to the cost of all the newspapers bought.

The Chancellor has made it clear that every effort will be made, during *our* change-over to prevent this kind of exploitation, presumably by the exposure of those firms and shops who take advantage of the transition period to make unreasonable increases.

In none of the three countries was it possible to make a clean over-night switch from one currency to another. The main reason was the impossible task of providing new or replacement business machines all at once, or of converting them in a short while. Fifteen months was the minimum period suggested for South Africa's conversion and although we may find it possible to make the effective conversion of machines in a shorter time, it remains one of the major undertakings in transition. By closing for a long weekend, however, all the banks and some other Government departments were able to open on the Monday morning of 'D-day' ready to do business in the new currency.

But another factor upset the careful plans which had preceded South Africa's 'D-day'. It had been assumed that, since it was not necessary to print new bank notes and there was no immediate need to provide more silver coins, that the provision of 30 million bronze coins would be adequate. The snag was threefold in its effect. Firstly, human nature being what it is, there was a certain amount of novelty hoarding of the new coins. I expect small boys vied with each other to see how many of these shiny new coins they could collect in the shortest possible time; but I do not suppose that it was only the children who decided they would like to keep some of the newly-issued coins. Secondly, these bronze coins did not get into active circulation throughout the country as quickly as had been hoped, presumably due partly to the vast distances and limited communications in some areas. This meant that there was a serious shortage of the new coins, despite the minting of an extra five million which were available on top of the thirty million estimated. Thirdly, it became apparent that more firms were able to change-over to the new currency earlier than had been thought possible. This meant that not only would more bronze coins be needed, but that the silver coins would have to be produced in bulk to prevent novelty hoarding of these too, which would remove them from active circulation in the same way as it had the new bronze coins.

Immediate steps were taken by the South African Mint to overcome this unanticipated difficulty by increasing substantially the output of bronze coins. By the end of May 1961, the number of bronze coins put into circulation had reached the staggering total of 75 million, only to be increased again to 100 million by September 30th of the same year—more than three times the number of coins that had been originally thought to be adequate.

In this country, the Royal Mint will be pressing ahead with the provision of no less than 9,000 million by our own 'D-day' in February 1971. It looks as if we do not intend to find ourselves in this dilemma, even though we shall have to replace more coins. Only the equivalent coins for the shilling and florin will continue to be of the same weight, value and size as at present.

One is left wondering, however, just how such vast quantities of new coins can be stored until they are needed. The banks may be able to help, or perhaps there is some secret underground super-vault that could take them all.

During the year preceding May 1966 the new range of South African decimal money was phased in. This differs significantly from the temporary currency described earlier. There are now only three banknotes—R1, R5 and R10. It is interesting to note that the R2 note which was a feature of the transition is disappearing. One reason for this might be to prevent associability with the old £1 which it equalled in value. No doubt old people, in particular, would have continued to call the R2 'a pound' if it had been allowed to persist. The three surviving notes are smaller than the old ones and have been redesigned in new colours.

Silver coins are very expensive to produce and by producing all their new 'white' coins in nickel the South African government could save up to R16 million on retrieval of the silver. This is given as the main reason for changing to nickel for the majority of the new 'white' coins. The only silver coin now being minted is the 1 Rand and this is already becoming in short supply because of its high intrinsic value. The other 'white' coins—four in number, 50*c*, 20*c*, 10*c*, and 5*c*—are minted in nickel and are smaller in size than the clumsier coinage they replace. The unpopular silver 2½*c* coin has now been replaced by a bronze 2 cent piece. This, with the other bronze coin for 1 cent completes the present range of South Africa's decimal coins. It has not yet been decided whether South Africa, with her 10*s* unit, will avail itself of this opportunity to be completely rid of fractional coins by phasing out the half-cent coin.

So much of our planning and transition towards decimal currency can best be appreciated by comparison with South Africa that I am going into more detail now than will be necessary when we consider Australia and New Zealand. Both these countries were themselves able to draw on the earlier experience of South Africa in the formulation and execution of their plans and so we shall only need to note the significant differences when we take a look at how Australia and New Zealand have progressed.

We will look briefly, then, at the publicity campaign which preceded South Africa's change-over, since we all will soon be subject to the same sort of intensive mass publicity and wholesale re-education in our thinking about money. No doubt the television will play an important part for us.

There was an added complication for the publicity men of South Africa, in that they had to provide literature which was both simple and clear and also had to be available in English, Afrikaans, German and quite a few of the Bantu languages. This all had to be distributed so that all the necessary information was available in the different parts of the country where these languages were spoken.

I wonder if, in our publicity material, we shall be able to achieve anything as novel and as popular as the rhyming jingle 'Decimal Dan'. This fictional character had his theme song set to music, and his propaganda was heard frequently on the radio, until almost everyone 'got the message' from Decimal Dan.

As 'D-day' drew near there was an intensive period of staff training, especially in banks, offices and shops. These were undertaken internally, since it was felt best that the needs and circumstances of each organization could best be measured by the companies concerned, rather than by a generalized approach from outside. 'Dummy runs' were also a feature of life for Stock Exchange employees, and the banks arranged 'familiarization' courses.

Conversion tables were issued, but as only amounts below a shilling had no exact equivalents in the new currency, it was really only necessary to get to know your way around this sort of table:

Old pence:	1	2	3	4	5	6	7	8	9	10	11	12
Popular table	1	2	2½	3	4	5	6	7	7½	8	9	10
Banking table (no fractional coins)	1	2	3	3	4	5	6	7	7	8	9	10

The 3*d*, and its multiples 6*d* and 9*d* could be converted exactly into 2½ cents, 5 cents and 7½ cents respectively, but the other adjustments tended to cancel each other out. By combining two fractional coins, these could be banked, as we do now with our halfpennies. It seems likely that when we also have a fractional coin—the new halfpenny—even though it will be worth

more than the present penny, we shall still have to make up round numbers of newpence for banking purposes.

In December 1961, Dr E. H. D. Arndt, the Chairman of the Decimalization Board claimed that the 'happy choice' of the 10*s* unit was amongst the factors that had accelerated the completion of the transition, because of the exact equivalence of the higher value coins, even the illiterate Bantu had little trouble in grasping the new arrangements. In his report Dr Arndt makes it clear that effective publicity and adequate preparation are essential for smooth transition.

Whatever conclusion you come to about the unit, and I would ask you to reserve your judgment until you have read the next chapter, there seems to be little doubt that the whole mammoth operation was regarded by South Africa, and by other countries looking with great interest at the outcome, as a very successful undertaking. 'There was no revolution,' said one observer, 'for the operation was meticulously planned and skilfully executed.'

To link our considerations of South Africa and Australia, I cannot do better than refer to the enthusiastic report on *The Success of Currency Decimalization in South Africa* issued by a group of Australian bank and Treasury officials. This report shows that, from the Australian viewpoint, it was thought to be a 'most successful, painless operation'. The report mentions all the relevant details, including the preparation, the publicity, 'Decimal Dan' etc, and also mentions the inadequate provision of the bronze coins and the reasons behind this unexpected snag. Their conclusions indicated the belief that other non-decimal countries who may be investigating the possibilities of a similar change-over can be reassured by South Africa's experience, which indicates that a decimal coinage system can be adopted to great advantage by any country without causing serious disruption. One significant difference which we notice when we turn our attention to Australia's preparation for 'D-day' was the avoidance of the fractional coin. Under the 10*s*-cent system they chose 1 cent as their smallest unit (1·2*d*) and avoiding both the ½ cent and the 2½ cent denominations, they opted for these coins:

1 cent (1·2*d*) bronze
2 cents (2·4*d*) bronze
5 cents (6*d*) cupro-nickel
10 cents (1*s*) cupro-nickel
20 cents (2*s*) cupro-nickel
50 cents (5*s*) silver

When I am lecturing on this topic, I try to take the new decimal coins from these three countries with me, and frequently it is the Australian designs that are most admired. (See photographs, Plates 1 and 2.) I shall be describing the designs of all three sets of coins, a little later, and I find it hard myself to decide which set is the most attractive—which is a hopeful sign when we think about what our own new coins may eventually look like.

Australia decided that dollars and cents would be the best choice for the major and minor units, and this was also New Zealand's choice. An attractive green booklet entitled *Dollars and Cents and You* was issued to the general public and distributed in huge quantities as the official guide. By the use of question-and-answer, and the introduction of simple, cartoon-type drawings featuring 'Dollar Bill', the man-in-the-street was helped over all the problems and common objections.

Many of these objections and problems will already have occurred to you, and I hope to cover most of the important ones in the chapter on the transition.

One piece of doggerel verse, which we shall not need with the £ as our unit, which the Australians were invited to memorize, was written to help convert the pence to cents, and went like this:

One and two remain the same,
The only difference is the name;
Three to nine lose one, it's true,
And for the rest you take off two.

I have also been able to see the short colour film called *Dollar Bill*, which was extensively used for publicity over the past couple of years. Now he is so well-known and accepted, that few people need to see him in his film any more. In conversation with an Australian friend, I got the impression that the new currency was already so well accepted in Australia, that she was surprised to find anyone still interested. This, I think, is another hopeful sign for us.

The effigy of the Queen will, of course, continue to appear on the obverse side of the new coins, and it is a pleasure to record that the design used is the creation of Mr Arnold Machin, RA, of London, whose design is used for the new English postage stamps which have recently appeared.

In July 1965 the Australian News and Information Bureau issued a Reference Paper on Decimal Currency, setting out in greater detail, though not in so light a vein, the background to their change-over, the passage of the Currency Act 1963 by the Federal Parliament, and mentions the other countries involved in Australia's change-over. Of these Papua and New Guinea had made their own legislative arrangements, Christmas Island was already using a decimal (Malaysian) currency. The new coinage was also to be used in the British Solomon Islands, the Gilbert and Ellice Islands, Tonga and the New Hebrides. Australia's 'D-day' was fixed for 14th February 1966.

In addition to the green booklet and the Reference paper, there was a wide selection of other literature, giving such information as how to write out a cheque correctly in the new currency, how to cope with dual price tickets, how to train and prepare staff etc. In one of them designed for businessmen, the common sense behind a tolerant and sympathetic attitude to anxious customers is pointed out as a mutually beneficial exercise during the transitional period.

In both South African and Australian publicity matter (and later in New Zealand's also) the advantages of simplification for foreign visitors is underlined. Most of them will come, of course, from a 'decimal currency' country, and thus will be better able to adapt themselves to the new money. Even if the 'other money' has different names, and if it is worth so much less, or more, the process of converting from one decimal currency to another is far simpler than when one of the currencies is decimalized and the other is not. This is obviously true of both the occasional holidaymaker, and for the businessman for whom efficient and quick conversion in negotiating a business deal is of paramount importance. Though our main concern is with the school, the home and the shop and office, it is still true that many more of us are finding our way abroad for holidays now and will benefit ourselves from the changeover. In very little of the literature, is there much emphasis on the benefits to tourists, but this might well be something that holiday and travel bureaux will want to add to the advantages of holidaymaking in Britain.

With Australia having moved over to a decimal coinage, it is hardly surprising that New Zealand should follow suit though it is probably a few more miles away from Australia than you might think—have a look in the atlas. This last major non-decimalized member of the Commonwealth has now pointed the way for us even more clearly.

The New Zealand publicity follows the Australian line very closely, which is not surprising when you realize that they also chose the 10*s* unit; they also chose the same range of coins in the same metals. Already it seems to be clear that the New Zealand transition is following very largely the good reception which the new coinage had in South Africa and Australia. With three 'recent testimonials' in praise of the decimal, I do not think we need have much fear that our reactions will be substantially different.

One of the most intriguing ideas which the Publicity departments in New Zealand came up with was the creation of 'Mr Dollar' (first cousin of Dollar Bill in Australia and distantly related to Decimal Dan in South Africa). A 'Dollar scholar' scheme has been launched for schools, and those children who pass simple tests in decimal 'know-how' will be awarded 'Mr Dollar Certificates'. Perhaps we can try an incentive to learning the new currency in our schools along these lines.

Like his relations, Mr Dollar is a film star, for the Government Film Unit produced a 10 minute cartoon film. Mr Dollar is also a musical man, for he, too, has his own theme song set to the accompaniment of a fast rumba beat. But, although we intend to follow the example of South Africa and Australia in choosing a February date, as the slackest time of the year for many businesses, I quote the following passage from the *Dominion* of August 7th 1963. Mr Seath, the NZ Associate Minister of Finance said,

> At that time of the year (July) annual balancing is completed, and ledgers are generally up to date, and the business period is a relatively quiet one. In addition, it is convenient for the Education Authorities who will be able to teach the decimal system early in the 1967 School year, so that children will be familiar with the system at the time it is introduced.

In this country, we do not always remember that July is mid-winter for the New Zealanders, which might also help us to understand this choice.

The attractive New Zealand coins are described here followed by brief descriptions of South Africa's and Australia's new coins—a trio of countries who have taken the opportunity afforded by a change of currency to introduce attractive designs on their new coins. These designs however, were only selected by the New Zealand Government after long public controversy.

The one-cent coin, which is bronze and has a plain edge, shows one of New Zealand's best-known emblems, the fern leaf. On the two-cent coin, which is also a plain-edged bronze coin, you can see the kowhai, which is described as New Zealand's unofficial flower, and blooms on one of the country's few deciduous trees. The other coins are in cupro-nickel, and these three—the 5 cent, the 10 cent and the 20 cent pieces have milled edges, and correspond in shape and size as well as value to the former *6d*, 1*s* and 2*s* pieces, respectively. On the five cent piece an unusual creature is shown. It is the *tuatara*, so named by the Maoris because it has 'peaks on its back'. Only found on offshore islands, this animal is protected by law, and is thought to be the last survivor and descendant of prehistoric giant reptiles. Yellowish-green in colour, and resembling a large lizard, it has yellow spots, grows to about 2 feet long, and has a pineal (partial) eye. Maori culture and tradition is represented on the 10 cent piece, and features a carved head, as seen in traditional Maori carved houses.

Everyone will recognize the kiwi, the large flightless bird that appears on the 20 cent coin, together with a fern in the background.

When we look at the 50 cent coin we find a representation of Captain Cook's ship the *Endeavour*, and this coin, worth the equivalent of 5*s*, is distinguishable by an unusual edge from the coin it is gradually replacing, the half-crown. This edge is $\frac{1}{2}$ inch coarse-milled, and then $\frac{1}{4}$ inch plain.

Last of the seven coins is a commemorative dollar coin, with fern leaves enclosing the New Zealand coat-of-arms. In place of the milled edge, there is

South Africa

See page 33

New Zealand

See pages 32–3

Australia

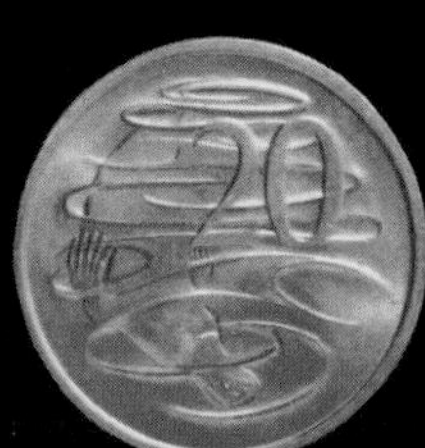

See pages 29–30 and 34

Great Britain

50 newpence
metal undecided

10 newpence
cupro-nickel

5 newpence
cupro-nickel

2 newpence
bronze

1 newpenny
bronze

See page 50

inscribed—or, more correctly, incused—the words, 'Decimal Currency introduced July 10th 1967'.

One amusing and unexpected feature of New Zealand's transition was the accidental production, through the use of a wrong plate by the Royal Mint, of 2*c* coins which were correct on one side but bore the words Bahama Islands on the other. Most of these were recalled as soon as the mistake was discovered but some thousands had already been eagerly seized upon by collectors and at the time of writing these coins were fetching as much as £70.

The designs on the New Zealand banknotes were kept secret for security reasons before their 'D-day' and now we can see that they are in fact, designs of native birds. The new notes are of 1, 2, 5, 10, 20 and 100 dollars—of which the 5-dollar note, equivalent to £2 10*s* 0*d*, is the newcomer though, of course, they all needed to be redesigned and issued with their values shown in the new 10*s* unit currency.

It is again, pleasant to record that the effigy of the Queen was designed by Mr Arnold Machin RA of London, and the designs for the reverse of the commemorative dollar coin was also the work of a British artist, Mr William Gardner ARCA, FSIA, of Wittersham, Kent.

The South African coins, as we have mentioned earlier, have on them the head of Jan van Riebeeck, the first commander of the Cape when it was established in 1652 as a victualling station for ships of the Dutch East India company. The reverse sides of the new coins have a variety of pleasing designs and represent the work, not of one, but of three South African artists—Miss Cynthia Letty, Mr Jan van Zyl and Mr Dick Findlay.

The 1 Rand shows South Africa's national animal, the springbok; the 50*c* coin has three flowers, the white arum lily on the left, the blue agapanthus in the centre and the orange strelizia on the right—an interesting choice since these three colours white, blue and orange are the colours of the South African flag. On the 20*c* coin two varieties of the protea are featured, another South Arican emblem. This idea is also carried to the 10*c* design which shows an aloe, a plant indigenous to South Africa. The national bird, the blue crane, is shown on the 5*c* coin against a background of Karroo Koppies.

On the coat of arms of South Africa, the state of Natal is represented by the black wildebeest, and it is not therefore surprising to find this animal used in the design of the 2*c* piece. What turned out eventually to be the smallest coin, the 1*c* shows two sparrows. The explanation for this design, the only one not depicting something exclusively South African, is from the Bible, a reference in St Matthew 'Are not two sparrows sold for a farthing . . . ?', said to reflect South Africa's religious heritage.

South Africa has two national languages, English and Afrikaans and this is reflected in the decision to mint half their new coins with the words South

Africa and half with Suid Afrika. Apart from this the only other wording to appear on the new coins is the face value.

On 1st April 1967 a proclamation was made authorizing the minting of a limited issue of five million commemorative R1 pieces with the head of South Africa's late Prime Minister, Dr Verwoerd instead of that of Jan von Riebeeck.

Turning to Australia's coins, we need some help from the publicity literature to be able to identify some of these designs which were prepared by Mr Stuart Devlin. The feather-tail glider appears on the bronze 1*c* coin, and the frill-necked lizard on the 2*c* which is also bronze. We might have called the creature on the 5*c* piece a spiny ant-eater, but we might have been told that we should refer to this animal as an *echidna*. Like the 5*c* coin, both the 10*c* and 20*c* coins are cupro-nickel; they show, respectively, the lyre-bird and the platypus.

On the silver 50*c* piece the Australian coat of arms is handsomely engraved, thus completing their set of six coins.

Only a few years ago, in 1964, the Royal Australian Mint was opened in Canberra. They were unable to cope alone with the need for new coins prior to their 'D-day', and were helped with supplies from London and from the branch mints of Perth and Melbourne. They should be able to meet the demands for replacement coins, since the new Australian Mint is able to produce at least a million new coins per working day if necessary.

So much then for the countries who have changed recently. Eire has yet to implement its expressed intention of going decimal, made back in February 1962. It may be that by the time this book is in your hands, we shall know if they intend to move across the 'decimal point' or whether our Irish friends wish to be the last stronghold of a system that has troubled most children and many an adult at some time in their lives.

I wonder if those who cannot bear the thought of losing out dear 'pounds, shillings and pence' are contemplating taking up residence across the Irish Sea?

You may say that, if all these nations have moved over to a decimal system, there can't be many left . . . and you would be correct. How many it is I do not know exactly but certainly there is no major nation that comes to mind. If you want a figure to argue about, then I will give you the one that is in the first sentence of one of my cuttings: 'South Africa has now joined the 145 other countries which operate a decimal system.'

The £ versus the 10*s*

By the time a few of my friends read this chapter, I am almost certain to get some rude remarks about running with the hares and the hounds, or trying to imitate the Vicar of Bray.

It is quite true that I have advocated the 10*s* unit both in public addresses and in writing, and I am very conscious of the fact that, unless this chapter can be made to sound very convincing indeed, it could easily be suggested that I want to sit on the fence.

Before we take a look at the reasons for and against, I want to underline what I have also said and written publicly, namely that the question of which unit to adopt is a *minor* consideration. The important thing is to implement the decision to go over to a decimal currency first, and then to argue about the merits of the two main contenders for the title of 'major unit'. This might tend to be lost from sight, for there has been a renewal of the arguments for and against the 10*s* unit. It is this sort of word-battle which has hitherto prevented the important decision from being implemented. Indeed, one of the most striking features of the Halsbury Report was the conclusion that the controversy over which system would be the best (or the better of the two main ones under review) had been the dominant cause in preventing an earlier decision to move over to a decimal currency. If this is true, then we ought to set out clearly the pros and cons, and then, even if we find that our views are still with the 10*s*-cent supporters, we should not allow our own opinion to prejudice the support which we should all give to making the transition to decimalization as acceptable and workable as possible.

I hope therefore, not to give the impression in this chapter that the question of the unit-value is the one and only important point. It would be easy to shirk the responsibility of setting out as fairly as possible, the advantages and disadvantages, by saying, with a fatalistic shrug of the shoulder, that as the Chancellor has made up his mind, and since the White Paper calls the decision to adopt the £ as the major unit a 'firm one', and the Government has a working majority, that it would be rather pointless to try and muster support for the 10*s* unit. That is not my view, because if I felt so strongly that the 10*s* unit was so markedly superior to the £ that any alternative would be unworkable, then I should certainly be using this space on the next few pages to press as hard as I could for the 10*s* unit. But, as I have already said, I don't feel like this at all—my earlier inclination (to put it no stronger than that) to the 10*s* unit was based almost entirely, in retrospect, on the *teachers'* natural viewpoint that one penny means more to the mind of a young child than one pound. A system then that would make the teaching of small money values easier, will obviously commend itself to anyone who has wrestled with shillings and pence. But we teachers, together with the others who handle money regularly in small amounts, tend to forget the great world outside where many things are calculated not so much in shillings and pence but in 'so many pounds-odd'.

We have already seen that there was division of opinion among the six members of the Halsbury Committee—with four favouring the £ unit and the two remaining members recommending the 10*s*-cent system. It is hardly unexpected, therefore, to find opinions also divided, not just amongst those whose work depends largely on their efficient handling of money, but also amongst millions of other people. Neither is it surprising that those whose main connections with money are concerned with the shillings and pence. It is natural that the junior school teacher, the small shopkeeper, the bus conductor, and many a housewife who likes to shop for small items frequently rather than have a large order sent once a week should all see immediately the great advantages of the system which retains an equality between the tens-of-cents and the shillings (50 cents = 5 shillings, for example).

In our turn however, we must also be prepared to concede that the banker, the larger insurance concerns, the man who buys and sells larger items, or who rounds things off in his mind to the nearest pound will prefer a system which keeps the pound as a stable major unit. That car in the showrooms will still have £675 on the windscreen, and the car-salesman will not be anxiously wondering if you are going to be put off because that sum of $1,350 makes it look much more expensive than it really is.

Actually, it was not just a question of looking originally at two equally-balanced systems. The Halsbury Committee investigated the claims of no less than 25 systems, and of these a closer examination was accorded not to just two, but to FOUR systems, the £, the 10*s*, the 5*s* and the 8*s* 4*d* unit (100 pence). Though it soon became obvious where the main choice must lie, it would be a mistake to think that no other system was looked at in the research undertaken by the members of this Committee.

Some of the most interesting parts of this Report are concerned with the reasons offered in support of the £-mil (£1 divided by 1,000) and other systems. It would also be a mistake for you to assume that I am blissfully ignorant of some of the other alternatives. An interesting, brief and readable case for

TWELVE as a more reasonable base receives the distinguished support of Professor Aitken in his *Case Against Decimalization*[1] though personally I find the case unproved, but you may feel that it would be interesting to look at a different viewpoint, and may like to read this evidence for a duodecimal system. I ought to point out, however, that you will not find support there for the *status quo*, but rather a scheme, involving new symbols for 10 and 11, and a monetary system also operated in units of twelve. As has been properly pointed out, we are not concerned to convert the rest of the world away from the almost universal ten, to do its arithmetic in twelves, but only to bring our currency into line with the decimal workings of most other countries.

So, to return to the opening remarks of this chapter, I heartily endorse the Government view that it would be wrong to let controversy over the choice of system delay the introduction of a decimal currency. Please, at the risk of repetition, can I ask you to keep this sentence at the front of your mind at least while you read the rest of this chapter?

I wonder if you will find, if you have been impressed with the reasoning for the 10*s* unit particularly, as I freely admit that I have found, that there really are some strong arguments for the £ unit, which were not appreciated earlier. If you want full details of the lengthy investigations into these rival claimants, then you must invest in a copy of the Halsbury Report or study the White Paper, in which about one-third of the contents is concerned with the arguments which led the Government to the firm conviction that the £ was the right unit to adopt. There is no attempt to minimize the arguments in favour of the 10*s* unit, which are quite clearly set out in these pages, although it is true that only a passing mention is made of the important fact that the other countries who have recently changed-over to decimal currency have opted for the 10*s* unit; whilst not retaining the phrase 'ten-shillings' but replacing this with 'Rand' or 'dollar', the countries whose transition we have been examining have claimed that some of the reason for the success of the change-over was due to the 'happy choice' of the 10*s* unit. But we must not be unduly influenced by this in deciding the system which will serve us best not just for a generation, but, one hopes, for a very long time to come.

One of the first arguments advanced, therefore is the drawback of changing the major unit. The sharp break in continuity with the past is stressed. I should have thought that this was hardly the most important point to bring forward first, but the mental adjustment in thinking about costs and prices and accounts prior to decimalization would certainly be complicated if the £ was altered, or if it no longer continued to be the major unit of currency. There is likely to be

---

[1] Published by Oliver and Boyd, 1962

economy to many business firms also if, in converting accounts to the new currency, there is no need to make any change to the £-numbers, but only to convert the odd money, the shillings and pence, in their adjustments. The arithmetic of converting the major unit, multiplication by 2, could hardly be simpler, but the retention of the £ makes the alteration of all larger prices, accounts and records easy. It is only the amounts *under* £1 that need changing —the main figures of the pounds stay the same.

This will naturally bring to our minds the controversy, which we have heard and read, about 'what to call the new unit'. Nobody seemed to like the idea favoured by Australia and New Zealand, of calling the new unit a dollar. We heard of Royals, Windsors, and some of the old coin names such as rials, nobles and angels, were temporarily resurrected, but of these only the rial had a face-value of 10*s* and that was way back in 1465 in Edward IVth's reign.

How easy, then to keep the major unit at £1 and continue to call it by the same name. It seems that no one can agree as to what a new unit should be called, although there are many who will tell you what it must *not* be called. So, by retaining the old major-unit, no controversy arises because you continue to call a pound a pound, and everyone knows what that is. It may be an odd line of reasoning, but it has a canny logic about it that must bring a smile to many a face and a shrug of disappointment to those who think it is stuffy, unimaginative or retrograde.

It is not quite so easy when you come to the minor unit, for, under a decimal system, whether it is based on 10*s* or £, you have no equivalent value for the coin that is one-hundredth part of the pound. Again it is remarkable to see that, despite the fact that South Africa, Australia and New Zealand chose the descriptive word 'cent', and we all know how many years, or runs, in a century, or how many men a Roman centurion had to look after, the word 'cent' is unpopular as a name for a British coin. I suppose that if our one newpenny is *not* going to be roughly equivalent to the American cent, and if it is going to be worth twice the value of an Australian cent, these are two good reasons for avoiding giving this name to our minor unit coin.

Although the reasons of 'equivalent value' cannot be advanced for the word penny, as you can for retaining the word pound, once again the only acceptable alternative is thought to be penny. Since the new penny will be worth 2·4*d* in our existing values, it must be distinguished from the old penny, at least until the disappearance of the old penny, and possibly for some time after the change-over period, it will have to be called the newpenny. It is hoped that, when we are all used to the new coin, and its actual value, we shall all start calling it a penny again, so that the 'new' part of the description can be dropped. Whatever our reactions to this *laissez-faire* in the matter of naming the new units may be, this decision is certainly going to please those who fear that all modern trends must of necessity sweep away all our hallowed traditions. It will, after all be rather pleasant to be able to continue to sing of 'in for a penny, in for a pound', to be able to offer 'a penny for your thoughts', or to listen to the children singing 'If you haven't got a penny, a halfpenny will do. . . .' Of course the idea of having 100 pennies in £1 instead of 240 will take some getting used to, but this may seem a small price to pay for the pleasure of keeping the familiar words of pound and penny.

It must look as if I am wholeheartedly 'the other way' by now, so let me set down five reasons which I have myself used to advocate the 10*s* unit and see how well they stand up to examination. I have argued thus:

1. With a 10*s* unit we should be able to retain more of our existing coins—down to the 6*d* instead of down to the shilling.
2. With a 10*s* unit, the 1 cent coin would be worth 1·2*d* of our present coinage, a realistic coin as the smallest unit of money providing a reasonable comparison with today's penny.
3. The 1 cent coin under a 10*s* unit would be comparable with the USA cent in value, and would have the same value as the cent in South Africa, Australia and New Zealand.
4. We should be out of step with these three countries, who have all chosen the 10*s* unit, presumably after looking at the alternative £ unit, as well as at other systems.
5. The pound unit must either use a minimum-value coin worth 2·4*d*, which would be too large, even in comparison with the present halfpenny, or else resort to the fractional coin—making non-standard business machines still necessary in providing a set of 'buttons' for fractional coins.

When you add the associability of the tens-of-cents and the shilling which I have already mentioned as a telling point for teachers, you may think that I have erected a formidable edifice to try and demolish. But, to be consistent with the aims of this chapter, you have now some impressive reasons for opting for the 10*s* unit, and you may feel that nothing I mention later is sufficient to alter this preference. Let us take them in order:

1. The coinage changes. No one has denied that under a 10*s* system, coinage changes would be fewer, but, now the details are announced it is clear that under *both* systems four coins will have to be withdrawn—the halfpenny, the penny, the threepenny bit and, almost certainly, the half-crown. Under the 10*s* unit, there would have been an exact equivalence for a fifth coin, the sixpence, and, in fact, it is intended that this shall be replaced by a 2 newpenny coin (4·8*d*). It was not possible to be very emphatic about this, since South Africa decided to introduce a 2½ cent coin to replace their tickey (3*d*) and under a £ system it would have been equally possible to issue a 2½ newpenny piece in place of our 6*d*, but the introduction of this

coin in South Africa proved rather a mixed blessing and has now fallen into disuse.

This is looked at in greater detail in the chapter on coinage, so here we may just note that although five coinage changes are involved instead of four in choosing the £ unit, when we turn our attention to the banknotes, we find that instead of *all* banknotes needing to be withdrawn, redesigned and renamed which would be necessary under a 10*s* system, *only* the 10*s* note is affected under the £ unit, and all the other banknotes, £1, £5 and £10 can remain unaltered. This, too, will be mentioned again in the chapter on the new money, but I find myself having to admit that I had looked at the shillings and pence and overlooked the pounds. The life of a banknote is quite short enough, 4½ months for the average 10*s* note, that the introduction of a new and elegantly designed 50 newpenny coin might very well cause even this problem to be minimized or to disappear. The 10*s* unit supporters, however, quite rightly point out that in view of the short life of many banknotes the replacement problem would not be difficult or protracted, but experience has proved in South Africa that the mental image of the £ is difficult to eradicate and 2 Rand is still thought and spoken of as a pound there.

2. My second objection to the £ system was that 2·4*d* was too large (even allowing for some inflation, or a rise in our living-standards) to be the smallest coin we should need. I was looking at the Australian system, where the 1 cent does, under their ten-shilling system, equal 1·2*d*. I did not take into account that we shall still have a coin worth 1·2*d* (the new halfpenny). I shall be mentioning the fractional coin in the fifth paragraph, but, as it turns out that the 1·2*d* is, after all, to be the smallest coin the force of this objection is diminished.

   With a £ system, it is certainly going to be more difficult to explain the parallels to children, since under a 10*s* system, the old penny and the new penny would not be appreciably different (0·2*d* more under the new coinage). Similarly with the halfpenny, if this had survived under the 10*s* system which seems unlikely, there would only have been 0·1*d* difference in comparative values. As it stands now, with 5 newpennies to the 'shilling', during the transition period, this is going to make the understanding of the relative values more difficult.

   But let the 10*s* unit supporters also realize that this argument cuts both ways. This close proximity between pennies and cents would, under the 10*s* system, make some people feel the difference was not worth bothering about resulting in a loss for them. For example—call 9*d* nine cents and you have lost the equivalent of more than 1½*d* for 9 cents would be worth 10·6 existing pennies. If values are clearly different, as under the £ unit, this ignoring of 'small' differences would not occur.

3. My third point involved, not internal comparisons, but external, and I think that this is still a valid criticism. South Africa, Australia and New Zealand have opted for the 10*s* unit, under different names. The value of our new major unit will be twice as much as theirs, and even if we try to overcome this by refusing to call our minor unit a cent—it remains true that the one-hundredth part of our new coinage is worth twice that of the countries who have recently changed over to decimal working. I am a little influenced also by handling money in Canada and studying the teaching of money processes, and in my limited experience of a decimal currency from that stay in Canada, my conception of a cent is that it is worth almost a penny using 100 pence—8*s* 4*d* as a very rough guide. This would be true in America also, of course, unless the exchange rate changes violently. So when they have one of their '$1·39*c* Sales' where a whole range of goods seem to finish up at this price or 2 or more articles for $1·39*c*, I would know that this was round about the ten-shilling mark (120*d* = 10*s*).

   I have been thinking of the minor unit throughout as a 'cent', not as a 'newpenny' or anything else; this was because the Halsbury Committee used this name for the minor unit and I naturally followed suit. It may be that some of the problems which would arise if we had followed the example of other countries in using the name 'cent' for our minor unit will be avoided by the retention of the familiar penny. This objection is also compensated for by the standing of the word 'pound' in the world, and, since we are not to have dollars and cents there is less need to worry about whether confusion over values may arise between countries on this system, as our currency will retain the pound and the penny.
4. I have covered the fourth point in the last paragraph—the influence on our thinking of the choice by South Africa, Australia and New Zealand of the smaller unit. This is bound to recur in the debates which will follow our decision for a 'heavy' major unit, but, as I have pointed out, their decision is tied up with new names for major and minor units. My anxiety would have been very real if we had opted for *dollars* and *cents* as names for the new currency, although I think the word 'pound' would have survived at least for this generation as a designation for *two* dollars, *two* royals, *two* Rand, or whatever designation might have been chosen for a 10*s* unit. Nevertheless as we are not falling into line with their nomenclature, there is less need to consider whether the values of our major and minor units must be the same.
5. My last objection concerned the fractional coin, which we are retaining as a new halfpenny (value 1·2*d*). It is true, as has been pointed out in the White Paper, that we are accustomed to the halfpenny, even though it has a diminishing value. Without anticipating too much the comments to be

made in the 'coins' chapter to follow, I have been impressed by the argument that, in providing for a decimal currency which is 'to last for a thousand years', the value of the smallest coin tends to diminish as wages and standards of living rise. The day is therefore foreseen when it may be possible to 'drop' even this new-halfpenny from circulation, being left with a new-penny as a minimum (twice the value only of the abandoned coin). If, however, we choose the 10*s* unit without a fractional coin, what happens when this smallest coin has no real value, and you wish to 'drop' it? You are compelled to drop a 'whole-number' coin, and possibly to have no 'one-unit' in your usable coins at all.

I have reserved until this juncture the large and complicated field of business machines, their conversion, replacement and streamlining. I introduce it here because of the conflicting reports I have gathered, revolving around the accommodation of this fractional coin, the new-halfpenny.

You may feel that it is outside the scope of this book to look at this problem, but I think you would be wrong. Firstly, secondary schools often provide commercial training, including the use of business machines, and this is likely to increase as the effect of the simplification of our currency will mean more machines in use, more firms employing the school leaver will be able to afford the cheaper and simpler machines.

In keeping with the trends in new mathematics teaching many pupils, even junior school children, are in many cases experienced and versatile in the use of simple calculating machines. It would be interesting to digress on to how you can teach children to convert £ *s d* into decimal fractions and work out complicated maths problems more quickly than by conventional means, even now. For teachers who would like to read about this, I suggest that you write to Addo Ltd, 85 Great North Road, Hatfield, Herts, and ask for the leaflet called *Dr Sterling: or, How I learned to stop worrying and love the Decimal.* With such an intriguing title, you may soon be tempted to write £6 13*s* 7*d* on the board as £6·679166—and you could then, *mentally*, say that 100 times this amount was £667 18*s* 4*d*.

But let us return to the problem of the machine. Some manufacturers claim that the extra row of buttons involved in producing a machine with room for this new-halfpenny, cuts the effective use of the machine by 5 times. Others claim that the extra cost of providing this facility on some machines—not all, for the banks do not work in halfpence—is going to be minimal and that the simplification which will be built in will more than offset the cost of providing for the new-halfpenny.

The best way I can illustrate this is by imagining an actual adding machine of today, and comparing its capacity now with its capacity under a decimal system.

Imagine a present day machine capable of registering amounts up to £999 19*s* 11½*d*, that is *three* rows for the pounds (hundreds, tens and units) *two* rows for the shillings, and *one* row for the pence, plus *one* row for the halfpence. *Seven* rows are now needed to give a machine a capacity of (almost) £1,000.

This same machine under a £1–100 pence (plus ½*d*) would have an equivalent capacity of £9,999·99½ newpence, *ten* times as much.

Those who support the 10*s* unit say that, if there was no ½*d* column, the seven-column machine could then take sums up to $99,999·99*c*—five times as much again, not ten times for the value of the unit is halved under the 10*s* system. But I am not entirely convinced that this is a fool-proof argument, because it assumes that it costs no more to provide an extra standard row of 'buttons' on the left-hand side to cater for the tens-of-thousands than it does to adapt a machine to cope with one halfpenny.

I confess that I am a layman looking at a problem without detailed knowledge of costings and all the variables involved. But, if it seems this way to me, and I have been interested in this for some time, and talked to experts on this, it would be surely more difficult for the ordinary man or woman to argue with the conclusions arrived at, and supported by those business machine manufacturers who have given evidence to the Halsbury Committee. *They*, generally, but not unanimously, conclude that the £ unit would make better use of machine capacity, and that conversion costs would be less also with the £ unit. We must accept this evidence, even if, superficially, it may not be so conclusive to the layman. This conclusion is apparently still valid even taking into account the extra costs needed to provide for the fractional coin on some machines. At present the provision of machines for £ *s d* working are non-standard in comparison with the decimal-based machines in use almost throughout the world. When we have a decimal currency, machines for ordinary calculation and money calculation will be virtually interchangeable. Ordinary adding machines (numerical) will, however, allow for a third decimal place (0·005*d*) if new-halfpennies are to be included in the calculations, thus limiting the capacity of those machines that need to take the new-halfpenny into account.

Standardization means easier power to compete in world markets in this increasingly important field, and if it is envisaged that even the new-halfpenny will eventually disappear, then full standardization will be achieved and costs reduced even further.

You will appreciate that there is also some division of opinion in this sphere among manufacturers, so we can only include what seem to be the relevant points, and form our own opinion. For those interested in the problem of business machine costs, temporary or full conversions and all the other machines involved I would again advise the reading of the relevant section of the Halsbury Report and the appropriate appendixes. It would seem that my earlier assumption that the 10*s* unit would make life easier for the business-machine industry would not be supported by *some* manufacturers. It is worth mentioning here that even South Africa, which for its population is probably one of the most highly-mechanized countries in the modern world, despite the adoption of the 10*s* system, did not at first abandon the fractional coin. In fact in their earlier proposals there were to be ¼ and ½ cent pieces. We assume, therefore, that business machines that are still needed for South Africa have only half the potential capacity which they would have under a £ system.

Before all this becomes too confusing, let me give one specific and common example of how some banks etc, will be able to keep conversion costs down to a minimum on some machines.

Imagine a machine of, say a million pound capacity; £999,999 19*s* 11*d*—no halfpennies on this machine. Block off completely the pence column on the right. To make this machine usable for the same capacity, but with decimal currency, the pounds stay the same, and the only alteration needed is to convert the tens-of-shillings 'buttons' to read, upwards from 1 to 9 instead of being, as they are at the moment all '1' (ten shillings). Once this is done the machine can still be used for £ *s d* until the changeover date, simply by putting the blocking-out bar over the 2, 3, 4, 5, 6, 7, 8, 9 buttons in the tens-of-shillings column, leaving the bottom one, the '1' exposed for now, and this bottom-button would be used to record any amount with 10*s* in it.

Machines are already being manufactured with the extra complete range of digits in the tens-of-shillings column, and temporarily 'blocked-off' as described above for all except the lowest button in the tens-of-shilling column. On 'D-day', this block is switched to the pence, which will then be obsolete, though the '6*d*' could still be used for the new-halfpenny for those firms who still needed to record them. The two 'shillings' columns, tens and units of shillings would then become available to record newpence up to 99. The machine retains its original capacity, can still cope with the new-halfpence where necessary, and the 'drill' is the same for the pounds columns. I know that this is only one case where conditions are favourable for such a limited conversion, but it does mean that not all business machines will be useless, or severely reduced in capacity on 'D-day'.

With this period of advance warning, and the surprisingly short life quoted in the Halsbury Report appendix for many of these machines, often as little as 10 years, traders and employers using machines of this sort will no doubt be able to plan the possible cost of conversion and weigh this up against the complete replacement of the machine, earlier than otherwise necessary,

pounds						shillings		pence	
9	9	9	9	9	9	9	9	9	11
8	8	8	8	8	8	8	8	8	10
7	7	7	7	7	7	7	7	7	
6	6	6	6	6	6	6	6	6	
5	5	5	5	5	5	5	5	5	
4	4	4	4	4	4	4	4	4	
3	3	3	3	3	3	3	3	3	
2	2	2	2	2	2	2	2	2	
1	1	1	1	1	1	1	1	1	

These two illustrations show how a temporary conversion can be made for a typical business machine of the type found in most shops and offices today. The major alteration is to change the tens of shillings to read from 1 to 9 instead of being all 1s. A mask is placed as shown in figure 1 and the machine is used until 'D-day' when the mask is switched to the old pence column, leaving the 6 (i.e. one-half of a shilling) to record new halfpennies.

pounds						newpence			
9	9	9	9	9	9	9	9	9	11
8	8	8	8	8	8	8	8	8	10
7	7	7	7	7	7	7	7	7	
6	6	6	6	6	6	6	6	6	new halfpenny
5	5	5	5	5	5	5	5	5	
4	4	4	4	4	4	4	4	4	
3	3	3	3	3	3	3	3	3	
2	2	2	2	2	2	2	2	2	
1	1	1	1	1	1	1	1	1	

The only other cheap way to use an existing machine after 'D-day' is to use only the pounds columns with the last two of these recording newpence. This considerably reduces the capacity but may be a possibility for some people. The ten shilling keys could be used to record new halfpence, but this cannot be regarded as a very satisfactory method.

and perhaps any saving they might make on trading-in the old machine—for competition to sell the new machines is bound to make some greater allowance over scrap value for this likely—and the question of tax relief on capital expenditure like this might also make a difference.

Not many of my readers may be concerned with the cost of replacing machines, and will not, therefore, be so directly affected by this complicated issue. At least I hope that I have made some people aware of the difficulties which these businessmen face. Ultimately I have to accept the findings of the White Paper on the subject and that tells me that, after all, the £ unit is better in the field of business machines and conversion costs. You may be disposed to argue that this conclusion is open to doubt, but it is quite clear that the official view favours the £ unit.

There are a few other arguments which have been advanced, which, writing from a teaching viewpoint, I had not fully considered, which should now be included.

If we choose to change-over to a 10*s* unit, we must *double* the numbers involved in our major prices (using dollars and cents in this example, for convenience) £798 becomes $1596. The larger the numbers, the more prone we are to make errors. Accounts involving large amounts, such as company annual returns etc, are already large enough to bewilder most of us; but it is a happy thought that you would only need half as much money to become a millionaire. We are used to a high major unit, and it is thought that, if other countries with lower, or 'lighter' major units were revising their monetary system, they would choose a 'heavier' system. This is, however, hardly borne out by the experience and decision of those countries who have recently changed, for they have halved their major unit. But with the £ unit the larger items of our expenditure or income would remain priced substantially the same, the train fare home is still just under £4 instead of over 7½ dollars, and we are not deceived into thinking we have a rise when the wage packet still shows, say £16-odd, instead of nearly 33 dollars.

'Associability' is a word which is bound to crop up sooner or later, meaning the ease with which we can adapt ourselves to a new system, or how well we can convert sums of money from one coinage to another and we have already looked at the easy associability between tens-of-cents and shillings under a 10*s*-cent system. But the important thing in such conversion is the ability to hold in the mind a firm yardstick by which the new coins can be measured. If we change both the major and minor unit, £ to 10*s and* 1*d* to 1 newpenny, both our yardsticks have gone. This might not be a problem for children who are only accustomed to smaller sums of money, but there may be unnecessary confusion if all the familiar guides have gone. Two important coins are being retained with identical weight, value and size, in the new currency, to assist in the transition. The 5 newpenny piece will be equal to our present shilling, and the 10 newpenny coin equal to the florin. Under a 10*s* unit we might also have retained an equivalent coin for 6*d*, but it is thought better to have a system which retains the £ as the familiar yardstick.

It is also thought that there would be more likelihood of prices being rounded up, and the housewife exploited under the £ system, where the 'jumps' are twice as big; but firstly, the Government has determined that a close look will be kept on this risk, and secondly, there can be no significant difference between the £ system *with* a ½*d* and a 10*s* system *without* a ½*d*, for in both cases the gap between one price and the next one (up or down) must be 1·2*d*. Adjustments by manufacturers in size, weight, or quality content is expected to iron out any price-differences that may occur. This may seem rather naive, but we do have consumer groups actively watching this sort of thing already, and it is doubtful whether any retailer or manufacturer would be likely to get away with this sort of manoeuvre unnoticed for very long.

But for the purposes of this chapter, in deciding the rival merits of the two systems, there would seem to be no significant difference, in the possible inflationary tendencies inherent in either currency.

Finally, we do tend to look at this matter rather in isolation, and forget that if we choose a system which suits ourselves, but which other users of sterling dislike (they may have good reasons for their objections or it may just be a dislike of change from fixed habit or usage) then much of the goodwill associated with the £ might be lost. Powerful support for the retention of the £ was advanced by banks, insurance companies, and large shipping concerns. Since one-third of the world's international trade is in sterling and it is used extensively in insuring risks throughout the world in this country and many goods in world markets take their price-lead from London, it is small wonder that the 'international case' for the retention of the £ unit has been so urgently pressed.

It is admitted that, in a trial run with 'dummy' coins, it takes a little longer to become quick and accurate at handling the coins under a £ unit than under 10*s* unit, but the groups tested with the £ unit, became almost as accurate as the 10*s* unit groups after a little more practice.

Even though initially the 10*s* unit might be easier for schools, shoppers and those regularly concerned with 'shillings and pence', the experiments conducted by Dr Sheila Jones do not lead me to think that it is worthwhile making angry demonstrations or lobbying MPs to try and achieve a relatively minor and transitional advantage.

Having tried therefore, to balance out the pros and cons, I should not be unduly disturbed, in the most unlikely event of the 10*s* unit supporters managing to convince the Chancellor of the Exchequer to change his mind. Powerful reasons can be brought by sectional interests in support of both units, but the 'firm' decision of the Government is to adopt the £ unit, subject to Parliamentary approval. Looked at from a wider viewpoint than the shop, the classroom, or the crowded bus for a couple of months in 1971, this is probably the right choice. If the relative merits are so finely balanced between these two systems, and the Government's view is that there are practical, decisive advantages in choosing the £, then I, for one, would feel it to be a great pity if wrangling about the rival virtues of the system which suits our personal situation better were to upset the smooth progress towards decimalization. Whichever unit is chosen, someone is going to have a problem that might be 'the other fellow's' if the opposite choice had been made. I want to see a decimal currency established in schools and shops and everywhere else. I want to see this introduced too much to be unduly worried now about the unit, which brings me right back to where I started in this chapter—and I am in good company in this conclusion.

Two older juniors cooperate in working out the answer to a decimal currency work card. The bottle top coins are distinguished by colour as well as by the value painted on them.

Again working with the bottle top currency, children can be seen selecting cards, sorting out the coins needed for answering the problem, setting down the problem and its answer and checking the answers.

Plate 3

In this school 'decimal shop' there is a conversion table to allow children to check the prices and all prices are marked in both currencies. The children quickly become accustomed to the 'new shopping', an encouraging sign for us.

Plate 4

The new coins

Planning a new set of coins to replace old ones is difficult enough in itself, but when both old and new coins have, for a time, to circulate together, fresh problems arise. There is a size below which coins are too 'fiddly' to bother with, or which too easily slip through tiny holes in trouser pockets. Likewise, there are coins, like the double florin, worth 4*s* which had a brief, unpopular life in the late 1880s, that are too big for most of us to want to carry around. Add to this the recommendation that we are to say farewell to the only shaped coin we have, the twelve-sided threepenny-bit—I suppose it would still have been banished even if it had *ten* sides, instead of twelve—that all coins shall be round and you make the task still more difficult.

But you haven't finished yet—there's a little thing called 'weight/value relationship' to be included. When you take a £5 bag of silver to the bank, it is usually weighed, as is the 5*s* bag of copper and the £1 of sixpences and the 10*s* worth of threepences. In the case of the last two bags, as the coins are not mixed, but having coins all the same value in the bag, it should weigh just right if the correct number is included in the bag. But the bag of coppers might include some halfpennies, and the silver might be mixed, too. Yet the total in the bag can still be checked by weighing. This is because of this weight/value relationship between coins. The halfpenny weighs just over half as much as a penny, and the florin weighs twice as much as the shilling. If this was not so, every bag would have either to be opened up and counted or else we would have to separate all the coins and have one bag for each coin value—all the half-crowns in one bag, all the florins in another, and so on.

As I worked in a bank myself for four years, before turning to teaching, I can just imagine the chaos that the absence of this weight/value relationship would cause, not only to Banks, but to Post Offices, Transport Operators, etc.

This not only cramps the style a little when it comes to suggesting the detailed weight, metal-content, relative value, shape and size of all the circulating coins, but makes it wiser to limit also the actual number of different denominations of coins produced. All of these must be distinguishable by touch as well as sight, and must be sufficiently different from one another to allow a coin-sorting machine to be able to operate properly. This usually means having at least 1/16th of an inch difference in diameter between coins.

The Government proposes that the new coins shall be as follows:

Bronze with plain edge	½ newpenny (value 1·2*d*)	smaller than a farthing, but slightly larger than the silver threepenny piece.
Bronze with plain edge	1 newpenny (value 2·4*d*)	very slightly bigger than the farthing, but lighter than it in weight—twice the weight of ½ newpenny.
Bronze with plain edge	2 newpence (value 4·8*d*)	slightly bigger and heavier than existing halfpenny, twice the weight of 1 newpenny (4 times weight of the ½ newpenny).
Cupro-nickel with milled edge	5 newpence (value 1*s*)	equivalent in weight and size to present shilling.
Cupro-nickel with milled edge	10 newpence (value 2*s*)	equivalent in weight and size to present florin and twice the weight of the 5 newpence (shilling).

A new coin of a metal yet to be decided worth 50 newpence (10*s*) may be introduced later. It will not be practicable to have a weight/value relationship with the other two cupro-nickel coins, otherwise we should have a very heavy, and unacceptable coin. But there is one snag that would be unavoidable. It means that the coin would render impossible the two-tier system of metals, which is easier to operate, and make a three-tier system again necessary. Nevertheless, it is felt that an elegantly designed 50 newpence coin of a size between the present florin and half-crown might be very acceptable. No decision is to be taken yet about the possibility of withdrawing the 10*s* note, which it would equal in value. The life of the ten-shilling note is short and replacement and distribution costs considerable, whereas even after a circulation-lifecycle of 50 or more years, the withdrawn metal coins can still be melted down and re-cast—and you can't do that with a 10*s* note. In my opinion, the

10*s* note is not held in such high esteem and it would be preferable instead to have a really attractive high-value coin in its place, perhaps incused (engraved round the edge) instead of milled, like the New Zealand commemorative $ piece.

Now, some of the omissions will become apparent. The Halsbury Committee recommended a 20 newpence coin (4*s*) but this is not considered by the Government to be a worthwhile recommendation, partly because the 4*s* coin was not popular back in 1887; it would be a very large and heavy coin, if it had to meet the requirements of weight/value relationships with the other cupro-nickel coins, and it is not thought that there will be a need for such a coin, even though the gap from 10 newpence to 50 newpence (5 times) is larger than the usual relationship between one coin and the next in value. A coin could be introduced of this value later if it was found to be desirable.

There is nothing to replace the familiar sixpence. We have already noted that the fractional coin causes problems, and the tickey (South African 3*d*) was replaced with a 2½ cent coin, which has now given way to the 2*c*. Similarly, we would have to introduce a 2½ newpenny coin, which apart from the difficulties mentioned would reintroduce all the problems of how to fit this into the pattern of weight, size and metal already described. The new coin (2 newpence) worth 4·8*d*—nearly 5*d*, is considered close enough to be a viable alternative. Obviously the 10*s* unit supporters are quick to point out this withdrawal of the 6*d* equivalent and to point out that it would not be necessary if the 10*s* unit was chosen. In this campaign they will obviously be supported by manufacturers of many slot machines and meters that now use the 6*d* extensively and who may find the loss of the 6*d* equivalent both awkward and expensive in conversion costs. Certainly the sixpence is now a popular and useful coin, but under the £ unit, the choice is between 2½ newpence (6*d*) or a new 2 newpenny coin (4·8*d*) and the Government has preferred the 2 newpenny coin.

The half-crown has gone as well, for very much the same sort of reasons. 12½ newpence would be rather a problem child for anyone, and would not be in harmony with a system based on ten. Again, the 10*s* unit supporters claim the half-crown could be retained (25 newpence) but in *value* and *size* the florin and half-crown are already too close and cause difficulties to some. The opportunity is being taken to rationalize the coinage by dropping the coin that fits less well into the new coinage range.

From the schools' viewpoint this question of distinguishability is even more important than weight/value relationships, and the details we have gone into in this brief chapter serve to stress for me, the complexity of trying to meet all these problems adequately, in many cases problems which may never have occurred to us very forcefully before.

The new halfpenny

In the table of values shown earlier, it will be seen that the 5 newpence and the shilling are equivalent, and also the florin with the 10 newpence. For schools particularly, this will be a most useful anchor, in handling some of the conversion problems in the change-over period.

There is no coin in the new range to replace the old halfpenny, and in fact the lowest value is over an existing penny. But the present halfpenny is fast following the farthing into the numismatic tomb. Ask yourself in how many prices and services is a halfpenny still needed or used. Before the First World War a halfpenny was worth something, probably about 2½*d* in present values, if not more. It is most likely therefore, that the halfpenny will be demonetized and withdrawn before 'D-day', probably by 1970. If we become accustomed to having no old halfpenny we shall, we hope more readily accept the lowest coin of a ½ newpenny (value 1·2*d*) when it is introduced, because its value will then be just a little more than our lowest *surviving* coin, the old penny.

The phasing of the withdrawal of the other coins (1*d*, 3*d*, 6*d* and 2*s* 6*d*) will be one of the duties of the Decimal Currency Board. This Board taking into account the advice of the Royal Mint and the other interested parties will suggest whether these should be withdrawn at the same time, or in succession. This may very well depend on how quickly shops are able to switch over to full decimal pricing.

But when the new-halfpenny (1·2*d*) becomes our new lowest-value coin, quite obviously many more of our shop prices are going to include this fractional coin. Here we have a very valid objection by the 10*s* unit advocates to the reintroduction of fractional amounts into a much wider range of shop prices particularly, than is now the case with the old halfpenny. A diminishing number of prices now include a ½*d*, and increases and 'special offer reductions' are often by a *full* penny or more. With a new minimum-value coin of 1·2*d* we are bound to see 'new-halfpenny' price-moves more frequently, with all the attendant error-risk in human totalling of accounts and change giving and the extra time involved in these processes. This is a most relevant point to make and one which the £ unit supporters might easily overlook. Because of this it is even more important that with all the notice they now have manufacturers should plan alterations in size, weight, packaging and quality to make even the inclusion of the new-halfpenny in shop prices as infrequent as possible.

It will already be obvious, I think, that, if 1·2*d* equivalent is felt to be small enough for our minimum-value coin, there will be no question of other tiny-value coins, such as one-tenth of a newpenny—which would be worth even less than the obsolete farthing. If the existence of the new-halfpenny is temporary, then we need not concern ourselves about other low-value or fractional coins.

Allowing for the disappearance of the 10*s* note, as we have already mentioned, one of the great advantages of the £ unit is the fact that all the other notes can continue as they are. Apart from being a big saving in banks, and of additional design and production work, the familiarity of the £1, £5 and £10 notes will undoubtedly assist in the transition period, and act as a prop for those people who might find the change-over difficult, especially the aged. Working alongside the 5 newpenny and 10 newpenny pieces (1*s* and 2*s*) the notes will provide excellent associability and facilitate the transition while currency of both types is in use.

One final objection which we shall probably hear, when it is realized that the new-halfpenny is smaller than the old farthing, is that it is too small. But other countries have small coins, some even smaller than the new-halfpenny, and it is not felt that our present large bronze coins are really of an appropriate size for their very limited value. Have we never been caught out, thinking we have plenty of change, only to find that on taking the weighty pile from our pocket, it is nearly all pennies? We are back again on this difficulty of fitting the size of these coins into a scale which will make it not only satisfactory for the weight/value relationships, and also of reducing the opportunity for fraud. If coins of different value resembled closely existing coins there would be the temptation to the dishonest to use the lower value coin in slot-machines and meters, or in making up larger sums of money for banking or change.

Perhaps, by the time this book is in print we may know what the new coins look like. A competition to produce the best designs for the new coinage was arranged late in 1966, and as many as a thousand artists have submitted their designs to the Royal Mint. If the revolution in stamp designs we have seen in this country in the last few years is anything to go by, we may be delighted with the appearance of our new coinage when it is eventually issued. South Africa, Australia and New Zealand all came up with some attractive designs with national significance, but largely avoiding heraldic devices and regalia and coats-of-arms. I feel sure we have enough that is traditionally British to give us a wide selection for possible designs.

The change-over

Nobody can say we have not been warned. Almost five years' notice has been given, in the hope that a long preparation period will mean a shorter transition period. Nobody is pretending that the transition period is going to be without its difficulties, either, and that is another reason for trying to keep it as short as possible. It has been suggested that it could be as short as six weeks. You may well ask why we cannot announce a day—one of the slack days, like a Monday in the month of February, 1971, and make a mammoth switch—immediate, irrevocable, painless.

Experience in other countries has shown that the main stumbling-block in the way of 'instant-decimalization' is the conversion of all the machines. If you imagine that this is not really a huge undertaking, you may be surprised to know that the estimated number of machines runs into millions—adding and calculating machines, cash registers, telephone-callboxes, slot machines, and I presume, the seaside amusement arcade owners will have their problems, too.

This, and other considerations, will mean that although the banks and some Government and other large organizations will be able to make the switch overnight, many shops and offices will be obliged to continue to mark up dual-price labels, or to continue to deal in the old currency until they are able to convert their prices, and their mechanization to decimal working.

It is most important, therefore, that, as soon as we can, we should all 'play' at imaginary decimal shopping, and change giving, and writing down equivalents in the new currency. If you are a teacher I hope you will find the suggestions in the following chapters a useful introduction for this. If you are a parent, you might like to be one step ahead of your children by testing yourself out on these problems. If you are neither teacher or parent, you will still be involved, and I venture to think you might be better able to cope with the transition if you do a little homework on the lines I suggest.

But, you may be afraid that you will be cheated during this transition period. Some sixth sense tells you that someone is going to take advantage of your bewilderment to charge you more than is right, or send you out of the shop with too little change. Most of these fears have been proved largely baseless by the countries we have considered, and the Government has also expressed its determination to see that such exploitation is prevented. The best way in which *we* can avoid any of this unpleasant possibility is to educate ourselves well beforehand. Massive publicity campaigns will be launched, leaflets and conversion tables issued, and every imaginable aid will be brought into use to ensure that *all* of us understand exactly what it is all about before 'D-day' is with us.

Planning this publicity will be part of the work of the Decimal Currency Board, and who knows what means could be employed? The radio and TV, certainly, and, if South Africa is anything to go by we could have a 'Decimal Dan' at the top of the pops in 1970.

Experiments with the normal housekeeping budgets, both with people of very limited income, and of an 'average' family (man, wife and two children) show that, even 'rounding-up' all price adjustments, the expected overall increase is marginal, consisting mainly in the purchase of several common small items like newspapers, cigarettes, bus fares, etc.

'Dummy runs' for the change-over will probably be a feature of offices and banks; there will probably be staff-training schemes in your factory or shop. The Royal Mint are now in process of moving to South Wales, as a step towards producing the 9,000,000,000 new coins we shall need. We may find that new stationery is being ordered and printed, and we can re-price old accounts for practice, or begin some provisional dual-price ticketing.

During the transition period in other countries, shoppers have found some articles priced in one currency, some in the other, and some with dual-price labels, so that the housewife may buy the goods in either currency, whichever is more convenient. Much of the housewife's early anxiety will be dispelled when she finds by consulting a conversion table that the shopkeeper's dual-pricing is fair and equitable. If small items are right and she usually shops for similar quantities, or with a fairly fixed total in mind then no awkward situation should arise at the check-out point, wondering if the total on the cash register was going to be a bit of a shock. In practice, it has been found that shopping and change giving is not as difficult as you may at first think. A couple of examples may illustrate how this can be overcome.

A box of chocolates is priced at 4*s* 9*d*. You could either pay for this in the usual way by offering, say 5*s* and getting 3*d* change, as at present, or you could offer the equivalent of 5*s* (25 newpence) and receive *threepence* change, so that you are still getting exact value and change. You will not be asked to accept, say 1 newpenny only in change, for, by this, you, the customer, would be out of pocket by 0·6*d*, since the newpenny equals 2·4*d* and not 3*d*. But similarly you cannot expect the shopkeeper to offer you 1½ newpence, because he then would be out of pocket by the same amount, since 1½ newpence equals 3·6*d* in present money. So, if *change* is offered and received in the same currency (old or new) as the price tag shows, no one will be out of pocket. It will not matter which currency is offered in excess of the price, in our example, the 5*s* could be 5*s* or 25 newpence, so long as the *change* is given exactly in the currency shown on the label or ticket.

Let us look at an opposite example. This time the box of chocolates is priced at 56 newpence. You will know from your conversion table that this is somewhere between 10*s* and 12*s* in present-day coinage. Count the first number, the five, as florins—5 × 2*s* equals 10*s*. So you offer 12*s*, or a higher amount, if more convenient, and receive 4 newpence change. This is the only fair way, since there is no exact equivalent of 4 newpence in our present coins, it being worth 9·6*d*. Neither 9*d* nor 10*d* would be fair—as either you or the shopkeeper would be fractionally out of pocket. You may think that these are trivial amounts, but the dangers are not in a small adjustment on one big item. A fraction of a penny would hardly be important on, shall we say, the price of an armchair, but on a larger number of small items, such as small household needs, newspapers, matches and some foodstuffs, this difference is no longer insignificant. It would be wrong to overstress this as a major hazard, because in going through the whole range of shop prices, and re-pricing them in the new currency, retailers may take the view that the losses and gains will balance themselves out. If the price of an 8*d* bar of toffee goes up to 3½ newpence (8·4*d*) then you will be losing 0·4*d* (old coinage) on the transaction; but if a 10*d* bar of chocolate is reduced to 4 newpence, the shopkeeper is out of pocket by the same amount, 0·4*d*. It looks as if we shall hear the expression 'what you gain on the swings, you lose on the roundabouts' quite often in the next few years.

You may think that my way of referring always to the new coinage as 'newpence' is lengthy and clumsy; I hope at least that it is not confusing. There are two other reasons for this choice also. Firstly, the Decimal Currency Board will be making coin-name recommendations, and, in the meantime, the Halsbury Committee's use of the word 'cent' has been replaced by 'newpenny' in official description, and these descriptions give no hint of a possible abbreviation such as 'nd' or 'P'. To invent one for the purpose of this book might, therefore, be both confusing and premature.

It is worth reminding ourselves here that, in making recommendations for actual coin-names the Board will be guided by the need to make clear that we have only a 2-unit currency from 'D-day', that is pounds and pence, not pounds shillings and pence, as at present. I expect that with the best will in the world, and despite the 'number' on the newly designed coins, many of us will continue to call the shilling-equivalent, the 5 newpenny piece, a shilling, and the 10 newpenny piece will still be known as a florin, or even 'two bob' for a little while, at least. Words for sixpence, threepenny-piece and half-crown will obviously fade out as names for specific coins, since there will be no equivalence in the new coinage for these amounts in single-coins.

One thing that I am wondering about—what will happen to the seaside landladies' 'guineas'? It is in this circumstance alone that I can see any small justification for our present guineas, simply because 21 will divide exactly by 7, and hoteliers can therefore quote daily prices pro rata where necessary, so some price-structure changes will be necessary there. My view, especially when looking in the window of furnishers' or radio and TV shops, is that the guinea is a rather mean way of suggesting a lower price, 39 gns is, after all, nearly £41, so we can all welcome the departure of that outmoded relic, the guinea.

There will be no need to take bank books into the Bank immediately after 'D-day', that is, if we follow the Australian routine in this matter, but these will be converted on the first transaction you make after 'D-day', when the account book can be adjusted.

Although six weeks seems to be an optimistic forecast, the transition period will probably not last the two years forecast by the Halsbury Committee. Experience elsewhere, and the long preparatory period leads me to think that it may well be considerably less. In any case this will be a period which will involve extra work for quite a few people, it will mean we shall all be carrying round two sorts of money, and—for the first month or so—we shall be taking out our little conversion cards to see 'what it's worth in the old money'. But these are essential temporary difficulties and will disappear once the new currency is in full operation. This may take a fortnight or so longer with the £ unit, than it would with the 10*s* unit, but this difference of degree is hardly significant. In any programme of mass education, there must be some who are willing to help put this across, either because their experience and abilities make this the sort of task that they will enjoy, or because the successful impartation of new knowledge is an exciting and rewarding challenge. It may be that this book will call forth a few who will be able to make a real contribution to the nation-wide acceptance and appreciation of the benefits of decimalization, and their services will be needed very shortly, certainly before we are all caught up with the complexities of the transition period.

I think that, in this chapter, I have covered many likely problems of transition, of a general nature, that have not already been mentioned in other chapters. Certainly, from my public lecturing, there are no other anticipated difficulties, which have been raised by parents and teachers. This does not mean that there *are* no other problems, or that new difficulties, peculiar to our own transition, or our own sphere of interest or work, may not arise; but, given the goodwill and patience of us all—there is no reason to believe that any difficulty will be insurmountable, or any of the temporary problems of the transition period will prove insoluble. It may well be a much less bewildering and shorter time than most people think, if reactions from South Africa, Australia and New Zealand are anything to go by.

No one is pretending that all the problems which all will face in varying degree will disappear overnight. But once we have become accustomed to the benefits of decimalization I don't think we shall think of this £ *s d* era as the 'good old days'.

But how much will it cost? The Halsbury Committee produced figures in excess of £128 million and indicated that for every year of delay after 1970 about £4 million would be added to the cost. It will be clear to you that I think this a price worth paying and that the seemingly high costs will be recovered in a short while. This will not perhaps be in direct money saving but in increased efficiency, time-saving, streamlining of commerce and simplification of teaching methods. These are intangible but permanent returns which will accrue very quickly after the transition. But then the original estimate made allowance for compensation which the Chancellor is not disposed to accept, believing that those firms upon which the cost of 'going decimal' will bear most heavily are those most likely to benefit from the change. South Africa estimated the costs of conversion at £9 million but the final cost worked out at little over £6½ million.

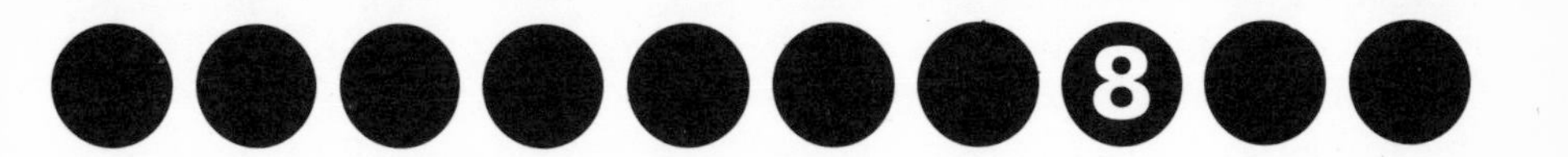

We already use the decimal

Some of our anxieties arise from a fear of the unfamiliar, the seemingly difficult, a feeling of insecurity sparked off by great changes.

If this could be said of the plan to decimalize our currency, we might have reason to look forward to 'D-day' with foreboding. In fact, some businessmen have already told me that they will be glad to have retired by 1970 or 71, just as if they won't need to spend any money in retirement. It is true that changes like this are likely to worry elderly people, and it is right that careful thought should be given to helping them. A little patient consideration for the 'old folk' will be greatly appreciated no doubt when they try to go out to the shops with their limited income in unfamiliar coins.

I should like to think that some of you are already getting some reassurance as you read this. But, by the time you come to the end of this short chapter, I hope to have shown you that the decimal already plays an important and an increasing part in our everyday life, and that we have only to recognize and use this to reduce the impact which the change of currency to a decimal unit will make on us all.

You must be aware of the first, and the strongest argument from my description of the child confronted with '12 pennies in a shilling' for the first time. We are born with ten fingers, ten toes, we grow up in a world which counts its years in tens, and hundreds. We have symbols for ten different number-values only, from 0 to 9. We may learn the Ten Commandments, which was apparently the right number for a simple illiterate Israelite to cope with. When we learn to operate these numbers, we are taught a decimal system, called 'hundreds, tens and units', and, as we have already seen, life under these rules was uncomplicated. Only when we found that there were so many exceptions to this 'rule-of-ten' did the little frowns appear and the real nail-biting begin.

But we are told that there are 2 halfpennies in a penny, and this will still be true, 2 pints in a quart, 2 stones in a quarter and 2 10*s* notes in a pound.

Then we are told that there are actually 3 feet in every yard, 3 bottles of school milk to make up a pint, and 3 teaspoonsful to a tablespoonful.

4 we are told, is the number we need if we want to change quarts into gallons, quarters into hundredweights—another misnomer, for it has 112 lbs, not 100—and, maybe, pecks in a bushel.

We may not have had to use 5 very often, unless we want to change bundles of paper into bales, but we will have come across it as an important part of an hour, 5 minutes, and had to recognize this on the clock.

6 may only be the number of balls in an over, at cricket, or perhaps the biggest number on the dice, and we probably don't need to know that there are 6 feet in a fathom, unless we want to work out just how far down Dad is buried in "Full fathom five thy father lies . . ."

7 days in a week we may need to know in learning about the calendar and the number 8 crops up in liquid measure, pints in a gallon, and as 8 furlongs in a mile, and 8 stones in a hundredweight.

9 doesn't trouble us until we are working out the number of square feet in a square yard, but perhaps I have written enough to show just how complex even junior school mathematics can be after the simplicity of the hundreds, tens and units of the infants' department. To be really exhaustive—or exhausting, we could take a look at twelve, or fourteen or sixteen or twenty, and sixty . . . and so on, but I hope you take the point about 10 being the first and most firmly entrenched number in our early thinking; to convert to a decimal system only one of our tables, the money table, is surely the first step in simplifying this complicated world of numbers that we have grown up with. Perhaps the fact that we can manage all right now, makes us unsympathetic towards the struggles of others, and forgetful of our own faltering steps in understanding, perhaps many years ago. But to argue in this way is like saying that because we first tackled washdays with a scrubbing-board, a dolly, a mangle and a flat-iron, that the modern home ought not to include a washing-machine, a spin dryer and a steam-iron.

But there are other things we already reckon in tens. On the television we are accustomed to seeing judges marking ice-skating and other competitions with decimal marks—'First judge 5·8, second judge 6·1, third judge 6 dead etc,' and we must have watched the ski championships, such as the slalom, and seen how the timing of competitors is measured not just in tenths, but in hundredths of a second—often a vital difference in deciding the winner.

More and more sporting events are measured in metres instead of yards, and we have no great difficulty in adjusting our minds to the slightly increased lengths of, say, the swimming pool, which has been built to allow for international events by a construction based on the metre. Many of us can mentally translate miles into kilometres, by the near approximation of 5 miles to 8 kilometres.

Dare I mention the measurement of temperature? We are experiencing a transition right now in our thinking about cold and heat. You may complain that you are not able to think in terms of Centigrade at all, and perhaps we shall not be able to do so until the Fahrenheit figures are completely withdrawn. It is surprising how easy this becomes if we fix a couple of reference points, such as 10° Centigrade = 50° Fahrenheit, and 25° Centigrade = 77° Fahrenheit. (Or, if you prefer it, to measure off the Centigrade scale in fives from zero, but adding nine degrees Fahrenheit on to the 32° of the freezing point, for every five on the Centigrade scale.) Here is a transformation to decimalization that we are already experiencing, although I think it would be more readily understood, and more accepted by us all if we had reminders of how to convert, say, once a week on the TV weather forecasts. Talking of weather forecasts, had you forgotten that the barometer is a decimalized measure; when you give it a little tap to see if it is rising or falling you are making comparisons in tenths.

The dashboard of your car has at least one decimal recording device—and maybe more—the odometer or parts of the mile on the speedometer are recorded in tenths of a mile, which is not how we divide a mile up at all in speaking of distances on a map or in motorists' handbooks.

Cooking temperatures are usually measured in Centigrade, and our electricity bill is costed on a decimal basis—kilowatts, as are the power of the bulbs —40, 60, 100 watts etc. The gas consumption follows suit being measured in therms, another decimal unit. From this you have only to look under the stairs for another decimal device—the meters. Perhaps we had all better learn again the decimal system on those dials, clockwise and anti-clockwise, for here we have scope for trying out the decimal in our own homes.

On the baby's cot there may be a row of wooden beads—a counting device. There may not be ten on the rail there, but it might turn your mind to the abacus or soroban. Using these simple calculating machines, based on ten, usually divided into 2 fives, an experienced operator can cast up a row of figures more quickly than many a machine-operator, and certainly faster and more accurately than you and I can reckon up a column of numbers or sums of money. Perhaps getting acquainted with a simple abacus might help some to obtain a facility in operating ordinary numbers, and consequently a decimal form of currency also. Well-made and pocket-sized abaci can now be bought for about ten or twelve shillings and there is a small, but rather expensive handbook on how to use one, published by Prentice-Hall.

In the schools, as well as in many offices and homes, there are ordinary wooden or plastic rulers. Many of these are marked out on 'the other edge' in centimetres and millimetres. We ought to begin to use these regularly, not just because it is a decimal measure, but because, if other metric measures in weight and capacity are to follow the conversion of our money, then we can familiarize ourselves with this at the same time. You can imagine a line 4 inches long, but can you imagine a line 10 cms long? In fact there is very little difference.

In the White Paper, mention is made of some of the new approaches and new concepts already being tried out in many schools. Because children are being taught to think in other bases, they will have less difficulty in accepting all these new ideas than many adults might experience. It ought to be underlined however that 'base 10' is the normal, and the one with which we are familiar and it is the other bases that are the new ones for us to experiment with. I shall not pursue this further as teachers will be familiar with this, and parents might not want to follow this up, particularly at present. But it is stimulating to note that the official view notes with approval the way in which a change to decimalization, and the metric system as a whole, will fit in readily with some of the progressive ideas on maths teaching now being explored in schools.

Much of the apparatus, counting rods, and equipment used in the teaching of modern mathematics will become even more useful with a decimal currency, and teachers will, I am sure, not be slow to relate the new currency to these aids already in use in thousands of classrooms.

No doubt, other decimal-based measures will occur to the reader. The librarian might well think of the Dewey classification system, by which very fine division of content in books can be defined, not only by the numbers from 000 to 999, but by a whole string of decimals after the point. For example the classification for beekeeping is 638·1, but for the keeping of silkworms you would have to look under 638·2.

In a local computer factory, I hear talk of nanoseconds, microseconds and milliseconds, tiny divisions of time, which are meaningful to the initiated, again based on the decimal. The only way one of these divisions could be explained to me was to try and imagine how long it would take light to travel a foot. If you have ever watched one of these computers in action, you may begin to appreciate what these fine, decimal divisions of time can mean.

At the time of writing the south of England is being subjected to a series of experiments to find our reactions to noise pollution in the form of sonic booms. The effect upon our eardrums is being measured in another decimal measure—the decibel.

Another very obvious example, which will become greatly simplified in understanding and teaching, is the concept of percentages—decimal fractions, or discounts, service charges, sale prices, commissions, investment interest, fluctuations in the cost of living graphs and statistics, royalties and a host of similar usages which give rise to some very awkward calculations.

The very phrase 'per cent' will be easily understood and applied to all money transactions with a facility that is not now possible. We shall be able, very largely to say farewell to the recurring decimal in money reckonings.

You, in your own sphere or trade, may be able to multiply examples of just how much we depend on the decimal already. My appeal is that we begin immediately to capitalize on all this, to bring centimetres into use, to make ourselves assess the temperature in Centigrade, to convert some of our trips in the car to kilometres, in short to have a good look around us, and ask ourselves whether there is not a decimal point lurking unobtrusively in many an unlikely spot, and, if so, to bring it from its comfortable obscurity, and set it to work in the task of educating ourselves into 'thinking metric'.

Wanted: a thousand beer bottle tops

This chapter describes a practical method of teaching the new currency, which has been in use for quite a considerable time already in the author's school, and which has proved a simple and effective way of introducing a decimal money system. It is neither difficult nor expensive for anyone to produce, and it is described here in the hope that teachers may like to experiment along similar lines themselves. Examples of the 1,000 graded work cards will be included, which are also used in the author's school to provide practice in the new currency.

I wanted to provide something tangible, something that the children could actually use as substitute money, much in the same way as we can already obtain plastic or cardboard 'money' for similar experiments and use with our present currency. Quite how I hit on the beer bottle top idea, I cannot remember, unless it may be that three of the children in school have parents who keep public houses. Anyway, these parents were only too willing to give me as many beer bottle tops, bent and otherwise, as I wanted. Let me suggest that an overnight soaking in some sort of pine-scented disinfectant solution is desirable; you wouldn't want unexpected visitors coming into school, literally to turn their noses up in surprise, would you?

By far the easiest way to convert these rather useless-looking tops into pseudo-coins is by aerosol paint sprays. They are more expensive than brush, paint and turps, but as one coat is dry in about ten minutes, you can actually transform these assorted dull bottle caps into shiny gleaming 'coins' of half-a-dozen different denominations in an hour or less. Follow the instruction on the aerosol, and have a few practice sprays on something unimportant such as the bent tops you have discarded, and you will be pleased at the result. I recommend spreading the tops on a newspaper, not quite touching each other, and spray from above, to prevent 'runs' of paint. Two light, quick coats are usually better than one, and will obliterate completely any trademarks or designs on the bottle tops, and, of course, will be free of brush marks, or bits of bristle.

Having decided what colours you are going to use for the different values, the longer, and more fiddly job of painting on these values must now be undertaken. But teachers who have used coloured rods will not need to be reminded that length and colour are associated easily by children. It is not therefore necessary to paint on the actual value on to all the sprayed 'coins'. The colour alone is sufficient, after a little while, to represent the value of the respective coins.

In the photographs you will see some children handling the coins working at the giving of change and using the work cards. In some of the pictures you will see that the children are using dollars and cents, a system which was in use before the White Paper was published giving the values of the new coins.

As I describe these two 'bottle top currencies', I hope you will remember that, as I introduced this just after the Halsbury Committee issued its report back in 1963, I had to devise a 'coin range' which would be flexible or adaptable to either a 10*s* unit or a £ unit, and I followed their lead of calling the minor unit 'cent', and the major unit a 'dollar'.

In the original cards I maintained this flexibility by choosing items that would not be proved an absurd choice whichever unit was eventually adopted. For example, 'a box of chocolates may cost 40 cents'. Under a 10*s* system this box of chocolates would be worth 4*s*, but under the £ system the same 40*c* box of chocolates would be worth 8*s*. Now, nobody is going to smile at either 4*s* or 8*s* for a box of chocolates, but, supposing I had priced eggs at 4 cents each? This would have been a reasonable price under a 10*s* unit, the equivalent of 4·8*d* but, as it would happen under a £ system, this same egg would cost you the equivalent of more than 9½*d*.

Now that we know that a £ system is to be adopted, we need not exercise the same caution in choosing commodities that would fit either the 10*s* or the £ price range.

Under the earlier system three coins were introduced only at first . . . the 1 cent, the 10 cent and the 1 dollar so that very young children were able first of all to spot the relationships of tens, as in the hundreds, tens and units of ordinary notation. Plenty of practice was given in exchanging the separate cents for a 10 cent coin and then ten of the 10 cent coins for $1·00 before we went any further. I also believe that it is well worthwhile spending plenty of time on the combinations between 10 and 20, as this is amply repaid in subsequent work.

One feature of the later set of coins we have introduced is the omission of any names such as 'penny' or 'newpenny'. This makes them even more adaptable in use for ordinary calculations or for money, and avoids a possible confusion over names—to say nothing of all the time I saved in not having the words, but only the numbers, to paint on the 'coins'.

After a firm grasp is obtained of the relative values of the 1, 10 and 100 (or dollar) coins, the other coins can be introduced, either one at a time, or in groups as follows . . . the 2 and the 5 cents, as subdivisions of the 10 cent piece, then the 50*c*, and lastly you can bring in the ½ cent coin, which makes a complete 'revision' possible of earlier work, but including this fractional coin.

The work on the graded cards is devised to include as many basic processes as possible, in all four rules and also in conversion of coins; when this is understood, combinations of two or more processes can be included on one card, and eventually quite difficult mental workings can be undertaken. How much written work and how much use of the 'coinage' is involved will depend on the teacher, but I think these must be introduced quite early, and become a regular feature of the lesson, so that early experience can be given in writing down the answers and in working correctly and neatly, and practice in handling 'money' in real-life situations is given. The children are encouraged to handle the coins even if they are quite capable of 'doing it in their heads'. To go through the motions of setting out the various coins needed, altering and exchanging them, is all valuable practice, and makes for more methodical working, and easier checking if 'something goes wrong'.

You will already have noted I am sure, that there is only one variable in these coins, the colour, with or without the amount painted on, that this represents. There is no variation in size, and no significant or intentional variation in weight. I also assume that there is no difference in the metal content. Although this renders this system unsuitable for blind children, even this can be overcome by the use of a punch to raise Braille-type dots on the surface of the bottle top, in which case they do not even have to be painted.

At the end of the lesson, the sorting of the coins is easily done into the tray, as you can see in one of the photographs. As in a cash till, coins of different value are allocated to separate compartments, so this teaches the children the need for some sort of order, and also makes it much easier to pick out the necessary coins for a work card.

We have found that there is no need to 'push' these coins and work cards on the children, as they enjoy using them, and quickly master the basic skills involved. All this leads me to believe that no great difficulty will be experienced by children in converting to this new system provided it is sensibly approached, and the children are given free access to this sort of equipment and work cards, or other planned work in the next few months and years.

At present both the dollar–cent set and the newpenny set are in use in school, and gradually the former will be withdrawn. It will then be later reintroduced to the older children as a 'foreign' currency, thus underlining the advantages of 'their money being much like ours'.

Instead of the $1 coins of the former set, we are substituting some £1 notes made from thin cardboard. I must point out that, as the £ is to remain the same, we have tended in the new work cards to concentrate on calculations below the pound rather than above. We have already observed that the choice of the 10*s* unit would have made the small transactions easier so there must be, in the classrooms at least, plenty of practice in the small amounts, that is those involving newpence rather than pounds.

Understanding is also helped by the setting up of a 'Decimal Shop' in the school in which fifty or sixty common grocery items are priced in decimal currency or given dual-price tickets and paid for with the bottle top coins. This serves as a useful introduction to the conversion and makes possible the check which housewives will be able to make for themselves about fair pricing under the new system. (See photographs, Plates 7 and 8.) Other similar applications will occur to many readers. How many bottle tops you will need will depend on whether the equipment is going to be used by several groups or classes at the same time, or whether its use is limited to 'money' or not. But, as it is so easy to spray up to two or three hundred of one colour at a time, it is hardly worth worrying about having too many painted, unless you are desperately short of storage space. They can be stored in plastic bags—one for each denomination or in a tray with divisions. I do not mind if they get chipped or knocked about, as it means they are being fully used, and with a bag of spares, it does not take long to 'withdraw' defaced coins and replace them.

It now remains for me to give some examples of a few of the work cards and leave you to experiment. I will include different examples of varied processes, mainly of a moderate or more difficult type, as these will be a little more interesting to read. These are not intended to be exhaustive, neither is it suggested that this is necessarily a good order, so I shall omit the card numbers. I hope, however, that any teacher who uses these examples will be able to see how this can be extended and adapted for use in their own classroom circumstances and according to present needs. I will give all the examples in newpence and not in the earlier dollars and cents system. The complete set of cards covers as many processes as possible, and, including revision work, total a thousand, grouped in a hundred sets of ten. This means that the same type of problems will be on all cards from 1 to 10, and another type on cards 11 to 20 and so on.

In devising this set of cards, the children are only introduced at first to two coins, namely the 1 newpenny and 10 newpenny coins. Only when they are able to manipulate these easily, in addition, subtraction, multiplication and division are other coins introduced, the 5 newpence, the 50 newpence, the £, the 2 newpence, and then the ½ newpence. Allowance needs to be made for revision, for presenting the same type of question as a mechanical calculation but more frequently as a short 'real-life' problem. Experience of change giving and conversion of coinage is included, and multiple questions in which two or more processes are involved. Problems of insufficient money for purchases, wrong change, averages and progressions, unequal sharing, and alternative ways of showing the same sum of money are also included; questions involving pocket money, minimum numbers of coins for certain amounts, proportion, percentages and fractions are touched on, though some of these examples are limited in difficulty because these cards are designed for junior school use. It will not be beyond teachers' ingenuity to augment or adapt this to suit themselves, although the complete set of one thousand examples will, if worked through systematically, cover most of the basic manipulations in our new coinage. It has not been thought worthwhile to include high value bank notes in these examples, nor to create deliberately 'awkward' amounts to test the skill of the brightest pupils; if they can digest easily the fundamentals of these quite ordinary money situations, as they may very well occur in daily-life soon, then they will have little difficulty in working out more complicated calculations and problems. Since the few examples that follow are included to illustrate the scheme, and not to form an extract from a school maths textbook, it is not thought appropriate to include any answers.

Specimen work cards

Add together 5 newpence, 3 newpence and 7 newpence.

Add three 10 newpence coins and four 1-newpenny coins together.

From 10 newpence take 8 newpence. What is left?

Share 14 newpence equally between Jack and Jill. What do they get each?

Today I was given 3 newpence; tomorrow I hope to be given twice as much as this. What shall I then have?

Add together 15 newpence and 18 newpence.

Take from 50 newpence, first 10 newpence, and then 35 newpence, and tell me what you have left.

What sum of money will I need to buy 4 bars of chocolate at 6 newpence each?

If I buy five exercise books at 2 newpence each, shall I have any change from the 10 newpence that I started with?

From the 44 newpence I left home with, I have spent 6 newpence, lost 8 newpence and given away 5 newpence. How much have I now?

What sum of money is exactly half-way between 56 newpence and 68 newpence?

Mother and Father paid 15 newpence each for their cinema seats, and 10 newpence each for my brother and for me. What change did they get from £1?

Show me 66 newpence in as few coins as possible.

Specimen work cards

Lay out 80 newpence in four different ways, without using more than 8 coins in any one pile.

Which of the following statements are true, and which are false?

Three books at 16 newpence each will cost over 40 newpence altogether.

£1 is not enough money to buy 7 toy cars at 15 newpence each.

You cannot show me 87 newpence in only three coins.

Half of 70 newpence is the same as 35 newpence.

The right change for a 55 newpence article from £1 is 35 newpence.

If I share 40 newpence between my sister and myself, we shall both have more than 20 newpence.

My bus journey to school each day costs 7 newpence (single journey). What will this cost in a week?

I have three Postal Orders worth 25 newpence each. If I cash them, shall I have enough money to buy 4 books at 20 newpence each?

What is the largest sum of money that can be shown with four different coins.

On leaving home, I had 45 newpence. I was given 10 newpence by a friend and paid 17 newpence each for us on the train. What have I left now?

How many times can I take 16 newpence out of £1, and what will be left over?

John gets 10 newpence a week, but Bill and Mary get 9 and 14 newpence respectively. What does that average out at?

If I start counting up in 5 newpence from 24 newpence—29, 34, 39, etc, what will the next three amounts be?

I have 50 newpence to share out between 5 of us; but I want to have 18 newpence myself. What will the others get then?

If 6 packets of sweets cost 18 newpence, what will 11 packets cost?

What fraction of 50 newpence is 35 newpence?

In a till, there is a pound note, 6 newpenny coins, and 3 50-newpenny coins.

I have a pile of 17 new-halfpennies. If I spend 10 of these shall I have more or less than 3 newpence left?

A small jar of jam costs 11 newpence, and a large one 19 newpence. How much do I save by buying one large jar, instead of 2 small ones?

I have bills for 55 newpence and 16 newpence. Tell me how much more than 70 newpence I shall need to pay these two amounts.

David saves 15 newpence every month for his holiday. In a year how much will he have?

Is 11 × 5 newpence more than 6 × 10 newpence or less?

Change the following amounts into Decimal currency:

13*s* 0*d*   6*s* 0*d*   2*s* 6*d*   15*s* 0*d*   19*s* 4·8*d*   7*s* 2·4*d*

There are four coins on the table totalling 20 newpence. If two of these are 5-newpence coins what must the other two be?

How much more is £1·50 newpence than 80 newpence?

Three ties together cost 50 newpence. If two cost the same, and the third one cost 14 newpence, what was the cost of one of the others?

Share £1 between 8 people equally (you may use $\frac{1}{2}$ newpence).

I was allowed 10% discount on an overcoat, which was originally priced at £7·50 newpence. What did I actually pay?

Halve 26 newpence, and take 6 cents away from one of the halves. What is left in BOTH piles?

Specimen work cards

How much change from 10 newpence if I buy 2 bars of toffee at $3\frac{1}{2}$ newpence each?

Eggs cost 24 newpence a dozen. What must I pay for 15 eggs?

'You owe me £4 all but 12 newpence' said Mr. Brown. How much is this exactly?

'If I had three more new-halfpence' said Harry 'I should have 50 newpence.' How much did Harry have?

Newspapers cost 2 newpence on weekdays, and 3 newpence on Sunday. If I am also charged 3 newpence for delivery each week, what is my paper bill for a fortnight?

In these pairs which is the greater?

50 newpence	:	12 5-newpenny coins.
£1	:	10 10-newpenny coins and 2 50-newpenny coins.
10 newpence	:	six new halfpennies and three newpennies.
13*s* 6*d*	:	65 newpence.
46 newpence	:	8*s* 9*d*.
17*s* 8*d*	:	88 newpence.

Divide 60 newpence by three and double the answer.

What is the smallest number of coins needed to show 97 newpence?

In the greengrocer's I spent 43 newpence. 15 newpence of this was on apples, and 20 newpence on oranges. The rest I spent on a small box of dates. What did this cost?

I changed all my money into newpennies. I had 4 5-newpence, 2 10-newpence and 16 new-halfpence. How many newpennies did I have?

The shopkeeper had to change his price tickets from the old currency to the new. What was the new price he put on these articles:

Bicycle	18 guineas	Saddle bag	£1 5*s* 0*d*	
Chain	12*s* 6*d*	Oil can	6*d*	
Reflector	4*s* 0*d*	Battery	1*s* 6*d*	Tyre 15*s* 0*d*

On to a full metric system

The section of the White Paper that deals with schools, makes it clear that the full benefits of the decimalization of money will not really be felt until we have moved on to a full metric system in all our weights and measures. It is interesting to note that in the specifications for the new coins, the weight and dimensions are given in metric values.

If you are unsympathetic towards a change of currency, it is hardly likely that you will have endured my enthusiasm for it to this late stage of this book, nor is it probable that you would therefore, look kindly on this very broad hint that the decimalization of money is only the first step towards a full metric system. It is evident however that commerce and industry are already moving in this direction, and, in fact, the metric system is already established in many branches of commerce and industry. Following the lead given by the President of the Board of Trade in 1965, many British firms are moving over towards a metric system, and in the next decade we shall undoubtedly find a great increase in the use of decimalized measuring. This is particularly noticeable in those industries who are keen to compete in the world markets, where not only prices but other specifications are measured in a metric system.

Perhaps you have forgotten the flutter of interest that was shown at the time, when it was hinted that we might be buying our vegetables by the kilo or our drink by the litre in a few years' time. I can remember the cartoons of harassed housewives and even one shop that had a short experiment in selling greengrocery by the new measure.

This progress towards a metric system cannot be divorced from the transition to a decimal currency, for they are complementary and the advantages brought by one can only serve to support the need for and the usefulness of the other.

It may be an awful thought to many to visualize working out how many kilometres your car will do on five litres of petrol, costing, say six newpence a litre. But, when you stop to think of some of the changes which we have already accepted over the past twenty or thirty years, this might not be at all a ridiculous calculation to expect from the next generation.

I cannot agree that it would be a good idea to do this all at once, but I have pointed out in an earlier chapter that we are already using the decimal quite a lot in everyday measurements—percentages, therms, kilowatts, the barometer and thermometer, many sports are timed and distances measured in decimal notations, and my old friend the hundreds, ten and units, of course—so that a further move along the decimal road seems logical and inevitable.

It may surprise many readers to know that the Ministry of Technology has had a Committee set up for some time, looking into the many problems of metrication in industry and that HMSO also publish a booklet on this topic (see bibliography). It would be comparatively easy to decide, for example that from a given date we might buy our curtain material in metres, or our carpet by the square metre, but the implications of such a decision would be so profound that it seems necessary to plan such a move up to 10 years ahead, to iron out all the difficulties of regulations, bye-laws, trade agreements and a host of other relevant considerations. Some of the measures used in industry seem most complicated and strange. In view of this complexity it is not surprising that industry and commerce are seeking to rationalize calculations in this way.

It is therefore, against this background of the movement towards a full metric system, that we must look at the decision to convert our currency in February 1971 to a decimal system. Once we have accustomed ourselves to the benefits this will bring we shall see more clearly the advantages of going on to simplify all our weights and measures by an eventual streamlining into a fully integrated metric system. This may prove to be the biggest step, but it is not one from which we should shrink any longer, for any further delay not only increases the eventual cost of changing-over, but leaves us out of step with the vast majority of the world's industry and commercial methods of handling finance.

Regrettably we cannot claim to be pioneers in this field, for even if you look around at the nations that have 'gone decimal' in the last century the list is truly impressive. More recently advocates of a British decimal currency have been greatly encouraged at the experience and ease with which South Africa, Australia and New Zealand have made the transition. Having made this historic decision, and having seen how many of the anticipated fears have been proved ill-founded, is there any reason to doubt that this is the right choice for us?

It would be sad, indeed, if controversy over the better unit for our new currency, which has hitherto prevented any positive action from being taken on earlier recommendations to decimalize, was to defer this reform, or make its acceptance by us all less whole-hearted and enthusiastic. The more positive approach now that the decision has been made for the £–newpenny system, is surely to pool our ideas, work out in advance all the ways in which everybody can be prepared for our new currency and, if this choice happens to suit us well, to turn our attention to the appreciation of some of the problems which this choice may create for those people, and those industries that would have preferred the alternative unit.

During the next two or three years, massive preparations will be going on for this great transition. First the designs for coins, and the minting of millions of new coins, with its attendant problems of storage and distribution; then the manufacture and selling of thousands of new business machines of all types to record the new currency, together with plans for temporary, partial or full conversion of many more existing machines from the great financial offices of the City to the cash register in the village shop, the writing of new, and the revision of parts of older mathematics textbooks in schools, and the plans of teachers to prepare not only themselves, but their pupils and, indirectly, too, the parents, perhaps, for the simplification that must result from the removal of some of the age-old problems of teaching this subject to young children. In this respect, it is hoped that some of the possibilities explored in Chapters 8 and 9 will be helpful and will trigger off some progressive ideas in the minds of many teachers.

Please do not think that, because we have all been given quite a long period of warning, that we can therefore sit back and just wait for it to happen, or ostrich-like, refuse to believe that it can happen after all. We, too, can use the time between now and February 1971 to develop and extend our use of existing decimal measures and concepts—percentages, Centigrade thermometers and metres, etc, and to familiarize ourselves thoroughly with all the literature and other publicity as it appears during the preparatory period. In this way we shall all be ready for no small change—in fact we may experience one of the best reforms of our age, the benefits of which we should long continue to enjoy.

Decimal quiz

1. When shall we change to a decimal currency?
2. Name the functions of the Decimal Currency Board.
3. Why should this book be slightly different in size?
4. Suggest some reasons for the failure of this country to 'go decimal' before this time.
5. Why should *ten* have become the accepted base for so many numerical and monetary calculations?
6. Give an early example of the prevalence of ten in calculating money or other weights and measures.
7. What was the 'godless florin'?
8. For approximately how many years did the florin bear the words 'one tenth of a pound'?
9. Were the Victorians consistently in favour of decimal currency or consistently opposed to it?
10. What was the double florin and why do we not have such a coin still in circulation?
11. In which year did the Board of Trade's Report on Weights and Measures recommend the adoption of a decimal currency as part of a metric system?
12. What was the Halsbury Committee, when was it set up, and how long after this was the Halsbury Report published?
13. Were the six members of the Committee unanimous in their recommendations? If not how were they divided and on what issue?
14. What was the recommendation of the National Union of Teachers' Memorandum with which I did not agree? What do you think of this?
15. What was the biggest problem forseen by the NUT and how was it suggested that this could be met?
16. Which other three countries paved the way for our decimalization?
17. How long has France had the benefits of a decimal currency?
18. Which neighbouring country has not yet decided to implement its recommendation of 1962 to convert to a decimal currency?

19. What is the biggest single advantage in making the change-over?
20. Will the new system be a three column system like the present pounds, shillings and pence? If not what form will it take?
21. What other advantages will flow from the streamlining of the teaching of money sums?
22. If, as a teacher, you had an extra hour a week, would you devote it to more complex maths concepts, or how else would you make use of this 'bonus' time?
23. Why was it easier to assess teaching time in Canada than in France, for example?
24. How long would you expect a maths textbook to last in *your* classroom?
25. Does the change-over make all maths textbooks obsolete?
26. Why is their 'life expectancy' shorter in primary schools?
27. What other factor is still likely to defer the production of maths textbooks incorporating examples of decimal currency?
28. When did South Africa convert to a decimal system?
29. Why was this time of year chosen?
30. What names did they give to their major and minor units and how do these compare in value with £ *s d*?
31. What is the range of coins now in use in South Africa?
32. In their original coins did South Africa drop fractional coins?
33. What fractional coins persist in South Africa?
34. Whose effigy appears on South African coins in place of the Queen?
35. Describe the designs on South Africa's decimal coins.
36. Did South Africa make a clean overnight switch to the new currency?
37. How did the Government of South Africa act to show that it was possible to bring some prices *down*?
38. But what common daily commodity was increased in price by 20%?
39. What is a 'tickey'?
40. South Africa seriously underestimated the number of new bronze coins they would require for the change-over. Give three reasons for this.
41. Why did the same problem not occur with the silver coins?
42. What special publicity problem will Britain *not* experience that was catered for in South Africa?
43. Who was 'Decimal Dan'?
44. Were the South African authorities pleased with the transition and did this influence any other countries?
45. On what date did Australia change to a decimal currency?
46. What system did *they* favour and adopt?
47. Name Australia's six new coins and their relative values.
48. Can you remember any of the designs?

49. Does the effigy of the Queen appear on Australia's coins?
50. Who was the cartoon character used in Australia's publicity films?
51. Has Australia any fractional coins and if so what are they?
52. How does a decimal coinage benefit a foreign visitor?
53. Is it true that over 95% of the world now use some form of decimal currency?
54. What other territories were involved in Australia's change-over?
55. When did New Zealand change over?
56. Why did they not choose the same time of year as Australia?
57. Are there any significant differences between New Zealand's system and that of Australia?
58. How have some of New Zealand's national traditions been preserved on their coins?
59. Did either Australia or New Zealand find it possible or desirable to make an overnight switch?
60. Has New Zealand any fractional coins and if so what are they?
61. Who is 'Mr Dollar'?
62. In what special way did the New Zealand Government encourage children to master the new currency?
63. Do you approve of this as a suggestion for *our* publicity experts to consider?
64. What are the advantages of using the words 'dollar' and 'cent'?
65. Why might these terms be unacceptable here?
66. How much do you think we should be influenced by the experience of these three countries in planning for our own conversion?
67. How important is the issue of the £ versus the 10*s*?
68. Why is it natural that teachers, shopkeepers, transport operators etc, should favour the 10*s* unit—at least, on first consideration?
69. How firm was the Chancellor's decision to adopt the £ unit?
70. Do you think he will be influenced by the pressure to adopt the 10*s* unit instead?
71. What is the main retrospective advantage of retaining the £?
72. What is the main prospective advantage of retaining the £ as far as prices and records are concerned?
73. Which coins would need replacing under the 10*s* system?
74. Which other coins would need replacing under the £ system?
75. How important is the *present* halfpenny and how do you account for its decline?
76. When is it likely that the halfpenny will be demonetized?
77. How many systems did the Halsbury Committee consider?
78. How many of these received more detailed consideration before the

main rivals—the £ and the 10*s*—were agreed to be the only real contenders?

79. What will the new major and minor units be called?
80. What importance do you attach to the argument that the adoption of the 10*s* unit avoids fractional coins?
81. How could manufacturers avoid including even the new halfpenny in many prices?
82. Is there any significant difference in the inflationary tendency inherent in either system if the minimum-value coin is the same (1·2*d*).
83. What coin recommended by the Halsbury Committee will *not* immediately appear in the range of new coins?
84. Will banks accept halfpennies under the new system?
85. In what way is the £ system superior when we consider paper money?
86. Do you think a 50-newpenny coin would be welcome in place of, or as well as, the 10*s* note?
87. In what way will the costs of compensation be met, if at all?
88. How is the similarity in value between 1 cent and 1 newpenny *under a 10s system*, both an advantage and a disadvantage?
89. What do we mean by a 'heavy' major unit?
90. What is the long term advantage of a £ system even with the fractional coin?
91. How important is the fact that major-unit values would have to be doubled under a 10*s* system, e.g. £695 becomes $1390.00—say in company accounts?
92. Why do the banks, insurance houses and shipping companies favour the retention of the £?
93. How important is the question of the international standing of the £?
94. Is the loss of the sixpence and the introduction of a new 2-newpence coin likely to be a serious problem?
95. Describe the simplest way in which an existing machine can be used for decimal currency providing its capacity is adequate.
96. Describe a simple way in which the ten shillings column can be adjusted so that it will cope with decimal currency on its introduction.
97. Provided that a machine is not required to deal with fractional coins, how will its capacity be changed by the adoption of (a) a 10*s* unit (b) a £ unit?
98. Are all manufacturers agreed on the issue of machine conversion?
99. How will the retention of the £ help those schools etc which use existing decimal machines by changing *s d* amounts to decimal numbers?
100. What is meant by 'associability'?
101. What is the 'life' of a 10*s* note?

102. Why do I describe the £ versus the 10*s* controversy as a minor consideration? How does history indicate that this would be a serious delaying action if pushed too hard?
103. Describe the suggested new coins—metal and sizes.
104. What changes will be needed in banknotes?
105. What do we mean by 'weight/value relationship'? Explain why it is important.
106. What effect does the fact that the old and new coins must circulate side by side for a time make on the planning and specification of the new coins?
107. Which two coins will be identical in size, weight and metal to two existing coins?
108. How will this be an advantage?
109. What do we mean by a 'two tier' or 'three tier' metal coinage, and which shall we be getting? Which coin makes this choice inevitable?
110. Why must all coins be distinguishable by sight, touch and machine?
111. What is an acceptable tolerance for a machine to 'recognize' one coin from another?
112. Why is there to be no coin of lower value than 1·2*d*, or put another way why is there nothing to replace the old halfpenny?
113. What do you consider size and weight maxima and minima for acceptable coins?
114. Who designed these new coins?
115. How many coins shall we need by 'D-day'?
116. Will there be any 12-sided coins?
117. Why are shaped coins not considered desirable? (That is any shape other than round.)
118. Would you favour an incused coin like the commemorative coin that New Zealand have adopted for their major coin?
119. What manufacturers and industries are seriously affected by or involved in coinage changes?
120. What temptation does a change in currency put in the way of some people? How can this be prevented or reduced?
121. How much notice have we of the change? Why so much?
122. What is dual-ticketing?
123. What steps can be taken *before* decimalization to alter accounts and amend stationary etc.
124. Why should most price changes balance themselves out?
125. How will the housewife know if she is being cheated?
126. What is the Government's view on this 'exploitation'?
127. What will be the names for intermediate coins?

128. What do you think about the possible death of the guinea?
129. Will bank books need immediate alteration and how will they be converted?
130. How long did the Halsbury Committee think the transition will last?
131. Why does the Chancellor think it will last for a much shorter time?
132. How will conversion cards work, and how long is it expected that we shall need them?
133. How can shopkeepers anticipate some of the problems of shoppers?
134. Will it take much longer for us to become reasonably accurate in handling the new money under the £ system than it would under the 10*s* system?
135. As most housewives know what they usually spend, how can they quickly decide if they are getting good value without comparing every price conversion?
136. Can you list some of the measures in which we use all the numbers from 1 to 12?
137. How does the decimal enter our lives in (a) winter sports racing, (b) international sporting events, (c) temperature, (d) cooking, (e) gas and electricity consumption, (f) a school ruler, (g) discounts, percentages etc, (h) libraries, (i) the car dashboard, (j) counting rods and other apparatus in schools, (k) noise pollution?
138. Can you think of any other uses of ten in everyday life?
139. Why use beer bottle tops for teaching decimal currency?
140. How can these 'coins' be distinguished?
141. How can they be adapted for blind children?
142. Which coins should be introduced first and why?
143. Why are graded work cards recommended?
144. Why start this year? Why not leave it till 1970 or 1971?
145. Is it necessary to introduce conversion into this method at an early stage?
146. Can these bottle top coins be used for other bases or for helping the understanding of other mathematical concepts?
147. Describe the 'Decimal Shop'.
148. Which measure do *you* think might follow the decimalization of money?
149. How is the way being prepared for our transition to a full metric system?
150. Are you now able to estimate (a) a litre of wine, (b) a kilometre, (c) a centimetre, (d) a nanosecond, (e) a kilo of butter? If these are difficult what other metric units are you familiar with?

Conversion Tables

Pence conversion table

old value	exact equivalent in newpence	suggested value in newpence	gain in old pence	loss in old pence
$\frac{1}{2}$	$\frac{5}{24}$	See note †	$\frac{5}{24}$	
1	$\frac{5}{12}$	$\frac{1}{2}$		$\frac{1}{12}$
$1\frac{1}{2}$	$\frac{5}{8}$		$\frac{1}{8}$	
2	$\frac{5}{6}$			$\frac{1}{6}$
$2\frac{1}{2}$	$1\frac{1}{24}$	1	$\frac{1}{24}$	
3*	$1\frac{1}{4}$		$\frac{1}{4}$	
$3\frac{1}{2}$	$1\frac{11}{24}$	$1\frac{1}{2}$		$\frac{1}{24}$
4	$1\frac{2}{3}$		$\frac{1}{6}$	
$4\frac{1}{2}$	$1\frac{23}{24}$			$\frac{1}{8}$
5	$2\frac{1}{12}$	2	$\frac{1}{12}$	
$5\frac{1}{2}$	$2\frac{7}{24}$			$\frac{5}{24}$
6	$2\frac{1}{2}$	$2\frac{1}{2}$		
$6\frac{1}{2}$	$2\frac{17}{24}$		$\frac{5}{24}$	
7	$2\frac{11}{12}$			$\frac{1}{12}$
$7\frac{1}{2}$	$3\frac{1}{8}$	3	$\frac{1}{8}$	
8	$3\frac{1}{3}$	$3\frac{1}{2}$		$\frac{1}{6}$
$8\frac{1}{2}$	$3\frac{13}{24}$		$\frac{1}{24}$	
9*	$3\frac{3}{4}$			$\frac{1}{4}$
$9\frac{1}{2}$	$3\frac{23}{24}$	4		$\frac{1}{24}$
10	$4\frac{1}{6}$		$\frac{1}{6}$	
$10\frac{1}{2}$				$\frac{1}{8}$
11	$4\frac{7}{12}$	$4\frac{1}{2}$	$\frac{1}{12}$	
$11\frac{1}{2}$	$4\frac{19}{24}$	5		$\frac{5}{24}$
1s	5			

Shillings conversion table

shillings	newpence	shillings	newpence
1	5§	11	55
2	10§	12	60
3	15	13	65
4	20	14	70
5	25	15	75
6	30	16	80
7	35	17	85
8	40	18	90
9	45	19	95
10	50	£1	100

Notes

† It is intended that the old $\frac{1}{2}d$ will be demonetized before 'D-day', but there *may* still be prices such as 1*s* $0\frac{1}{2}d$ or 2s $0\frac{1}{2}d$, in which case it is suggested that the halfpenny is ignored making the conversions equivalent to 5 newpence and 10 newpence resulting in a gain for the customer of $\frac{5}{24}d$.

* At two points in this suggested conversion table, 3*d* and 9*d*, the difference in values falls exactly halfway. By making $3d=1$ newpenny and $9d=4$ newpence there is a gain of $\frac{1}{4}d$ on the former balanced by a loss of $\frac{1}{4}d$ on the latter. It may be that the Decimal Currency Board will reverse this making $3d=1\frac{1}{2}$ newpence and $9d=3\frac{1}{2}$ newpence, but either way the gains and losses will balance each other.

§ To simplify transition, the 5 newpence coin will be equivalent to the present shilling in weight, size and value. The 10 newpence coin will be similarly equivalent to the present florin.

Bibliography

Report of the Committee of Enquiry into Decimal Currency (Halsbury) HMSO 1963
Decimal Currency in the United Kingdom HMSO 1966
Changing to the Metric System (Ministry of Technology: National Physical Laboratory) HMSO 1966

For younger readers
B. Elkin *True Book of Money* Children's Press 1960
From Barter to Gold Rand McNally 1961
D. Malbert *Discovering Coins* University of London Press

For older readers
A. C. Cope *Money* Ward Lock Educational 1959
A. H. Quiggen *The Story of Money* Methuen

T. Kojuna *The Japanese Abacus* Prentice-Hall 1965
A. Aitken *The Case Against Decimalization* Oliver and Boyd 1962

Teachers may find the following details of entries in reference books useful.
World Book Encyclopedia (International Edition) Volume 8; pages 377–83
Children's Britannica Volume 6; pages 472–3
Oxford Junior Encyclopedia Volume 7; pages 297–300
Waverley Books of Knowledge Volume 5; pages 233–6
Mee's Children's Encyclopedia Volume 8; page 5389, Volume 10; page 7318

Index

abacus *61*
abbreviations for coin names *56*
Addo Ltd *42*
Aden *23*
adjustments
  in prices *56*
  in quality and quantity *47, 52*
Afrikaans *24, 28, 33*
Aitken, Processor A. *37*
alternative systems *35–6*
American monetary system *41*
arithmetic, first steps *17*
apparatus in maths teaching *20*
approximation risks *40*
Arndt, Dr E. H. D. *29*
'associability' *46–7, 53*
Australia
  artist for currency designs *34*
  coins *29–30, 34*
  Currency Act 1963 *30*
  'D-day' (February 14th 1966) *30*
  'Dollar Bill' *30*
  publicity material *23, 30*
  Royal Australian Mint *34*
  territories included *30*
  transition *30ff*

Babylonian system *11*
banknotes
  designs *40, 53*
  life of *40, 50*
banks
  alteration of bankbooks *57*
  closure during transition *26*
  views on choice of unit *47*
Bantu *29*
bases in maths *19*

Becklake Committee *24*
blind persons
  distinguishing coins *49*
  pupils *66*
Botswana (Bechuanaland) *24*
bottle top currency *64ff*
British Association for the Advancement of Science *13*
business machines
  capacity *43*
  conversion *26, 42ff*
  replacement *44*
  standardization *43*

Canada *16, 19–20, 41*
Caribbean *23*
Centigrade *60–1*
centimetres *61*
cents *24, 30, 38, 41*
change giving *18, 55*
Christmas Island *30*
coinage changes (Britain) *38–9, 49–50*
coins, new (Britain)
  designs *53*
  distinguishability from old *49–50*
  estimated requirement *55*
  rationalization *51*
  shapes and sizes *49, 53*
  storage *27*
  weight/value relationship *49, 51*
Colonial Conferences *13*
Commerce, Association of British Chambers of *13*
compensation *8, 58*
consumer groups *47*
conversion tables *28, 55, 83–5*
cookery temperatures *61*

Index

costs of transition *58*
customer relationships *31*
Cyprus *23*

'D-day'
  Australia *30*
  Britain *7, 56–7*
  New Zealand *32–3*
  South Africa *28*
decibel *62*
Decimal Currency Board *8, 52, 56, 85*
'Decimal Dan' *28–9, 55*
decimal fractions *62*
decimal measures *59ff*
'Decimal Shop' *67*
'Decimal Quiz' *77ff*
demonetization *8, 52*
Devlin, Stuart *34*
Dewey Decimal System *62*
diminishing value of small coins *41–2*
'disenchantment' with maths *18*
distinguishability of coins *51*
dollar *38, 41*
'Dollar Bill' *30*
'Dollar, Mr' *31*
Dollar Scholar scheme *31*
dual-pricing *55*
dummy coins *47, 64ff*
duodecimal system *37*

Edwardians and decimalization *13*
Eire *15, 34*
electricity meters *62*
'equivalent value' *38*
Esperanto *16*
experiments with various units *47*

Fahrenheit *61*
familiarization courses *28*
farthings *20, 52*
Findlay, Dick *33*
five shilling unit *36*
florin
  double *12*
  'godless' *12*
foreign visitors, businessmen *31*
fractional coins *25, 40–2*
France *16*

Gaitskell, Rt Hon Hugh *13*
Gardner, William *33*
gas measurement *61*
German language *28*
Gilbert and Ellice Islands *30*
goodwill of the £ *47*
guineas *57*

half-crown *39, 51*
halfpenny *8, 39, 52*
Halsbury Committee *7, 14, 35–6, 44*
  costs of transition *58*
  Memorandum of Dissent *14, 36*
  terms of reference *14*
  unaccepted recommendations *51*
'heavy' units *46*
history of decimalization *11ff*
hoarding of new coins *26*
hundred pence unit *36*

immediate conversion, impossibility of *26, 54*
Imperial Conference *13*
inflation *26, 47*
insurance companies *47*
interest rates *62*
International Organization for Standardization *9*
international sport *60*
international standing of £ *47*
Ireland *15, 34*

Jewish measures *11–12*
Jones, Dr Sheila *47*

kilometre, kilogramme, etc *60*

language problem (S. Africa) *28, 33*
large numbers, error in *46*
Lesotho (Basutoland) *24*
Letty, Cynthia *33*
'light' units *46*
Lloyd, Rt Hon Selwyn *13*
long term considerations *42*

Machin, Arnold *30, 33*
major and minor units *37–8, 41, 46*
mathematics in schools *17, 19, 62*
measurement *59–61*

metal
  for coins *24, 27, 29, 49–50*
  value reclaimed *27, 50*
metric system *15, 74ff*
mil (£-mil system) *36*
Mint
  Royal (Britain) *27, 55*
  Royal Australian *34*
  South African *27*
Moses, Law of *11, 59*

names for new currency *38, 41*
New Guinea *30*
New Hebrides *30*
'new maths' *19, 62*
New Zealand
  coins *32–3*
  'D-day' (July 10th 1967) *33*
  Maori culture *32*
  publicity material *31*
National Union of Teachers *14–15*

overcharging *47, 54–5*

Papua *30*
penny (as name) *38*
percentages *62*
'place value' *17*
postage stamps *30, 53*
pound unit *35–42, 57*
price adjustments *56*
publicity material *23, 27, 55*
Publishers' Association *20*

rationalization of coinage *51*
replacement of textbooks *20*
retention of existing coins *39ff*
Riebeeck, J. van *25, 33*
Royal Commissions *12*

Seath, Mr *32*
Select Committee *12*
shopping *54–6, 74*
sixpence, replacement of *39, 51*
slot machines *50, 51, 54*
Solomon Islands *30*
soroban *61*
South Africa
  Afrikaans *24, 29, 33*
  Arndt, Dr E. H. D. *29*
  artists for coinage designs *33*
  bank closure *26*
  Becklake Committee *24*
  conversion tables *28*
  'D-day' (February 14th 1961) *24*
  Decimal Currency Act 24
  'Decimal Dan' *28–9, 55*
  familiarization courses *28*
  fractional coins *25*
  inflation *26*
  language problems *28, 34*
  Natal *33*
  other territories included *24*
  publicity material *23, 28*
  Rand and cent *24*
  Riebeeck, J. van *25, 33*
  transition in two stages *24–5*
  underestimate of coinage requirements *26*
  unit chosen *23*
  Verwoerd, Dr H. F. *34*
South West Africa *24*
sports, metric distances, *60*
stationery, replacement *55*
streamlining of monetary calculations *18*
Swaziland *24*

tables, mathematics *59–60*
Technology, Ministry of, Report *75*
television *21, 28*
ten shilling coin *50*
ten shilling note *40, 50, 53*
ten shilling unit *35–42, 57*
textbooks
  French *16*
  replacement and costs *15, 20–1*
thousand (£-mil unit) *36*
'tickey' *25*
time saving in school work *19*
tithes *11*
tolerance between coin sizes *50*
Tonga *30*
tourists, benefits for *31*
transition, phasing of (Britain) *57*
transitional difficulties *21, 54–8*
two-tier system
  metal *50*
  written *18, 56*

Index

unit, choice of *34–42*

Verwoerd, Dr H. F. *34*
Victorians and decimalization *12*

weights and measures *59ff*
  Board of Trade Report on *13*
weight/value relationship *49, 51*

West Indies *23*
withdrawal of existing coinage *52*
work cards *67, 69ff*

Zamenhof *16*
zero *17*
Zyl, J. van *33*